To Our Readers

Changes: Readers of this publication are encouraged to submit suggestions and changes that will improve it. Recommendations may be sent directly to Commanding General, Marine Corps Combat Development Command, Doctrine Division (C 42), 3300 Russell Road, Suite 318A, Quantico, VA 22134-5021 or by fax to 703-784-2917 (DSN 278-2917) or by E-mail to **morgannc@mccdc.usmc.mil**. Recommendations should include the following information:

- Location of change
     Publication number and title
     Current page number
     Paragraph number (if applicable)
     Line number
     Figure or table number (if applicable)
- Nature of change
     Add, delete
     Proposed new text, preferably double-spaced and typewritten
- Justification and/or source of change

Additional copies: A printed copy of this publication may be obtained from Marine Corps Logistics Base, Albany, GA 31704-5001, by following the instructions in MCBul 5600, *Marine Corps Doctrinal Publications Status.* An electronic copy may be obtained from the Doctrine Division, MCCDC, world wide web home page which is found at the following universal reference locator: **http://www.doctrine.usmc.mil**.

DEPARTMENT OF THE NAVY
Headquarters United States Marine Corps
Washington, D.C. 20380-1775

13 August 2003

FOREWORD

Helicopter rope suspension techniques (HRST) provide Marines with the ability to conduct helicopter insertions and extractions where helicopter landings are impractical. Marine Corps Reference Publication (MCRP) 3-11.4A, *Helicopter Rope Suspension Techniques (HRST) Operations*, establishes standards; serves as a guide for the realistic and safe training of Marines in HRST skills; and outlines the techniques, procedures, and equipment used to perform HRST. It is not intended to teach the basics of rope training or the basics of rappelling as they apply to cliff assault.

MCRP 3-11.4A applies to all Marines involved in HRST operations. It delineates responsibilities among aircrews and HRST personnel regarding the installation and maintenance of HRST equipment and the procedures required to conduct HRST operations. To enhance interoperability, the HRST rigging procedures for helicopters from other Services have been included in this publication.

This publication supersedes Fleet Marine Force Manual (FMFM) 7-40, *Helicopter Insertion/Extraction*, dated 11 May 1992.

Reviewed and approved this date.

BY DIRECTION OF THE COMMANDANT OF THE MARINE CORPS

EDWARD HANLON, JR.
Lieutenant General, U.S. Marine Corps
Commanding General
Marine Corps Combat Development Command

Publication Control Number: 144 000108 00

Helicopter Rope Suspension Techniques (HRST) Operations

Table of Contents

Chapter 1. Introduction

Chapter 2. Ropes, Equipment, and Knots

Chapter 3. Tower Training

Chapter 4. Helicopter Rappelling Operations

Chapter 5. Fast Rope Operations

Chapter 6. Special Patrol Insertion and Extraction Operations

Chapter 7. Jacob's Ladder Operations

Appendices

CHAPTER 1
INTRODUCTION

Helicopter rope suspension techniques (HRST) is a high-risk operation that can be conducted safely if the contents of this publication are adhered to and current directives are followed. Noncompliance with this publication or current directives and any unauthorized modifications or installation of unauthorized HRST equipment can result in injury or death to personnel and/or damage to equipment.

Note: This term, HRST, modifies the existing term and is approved for inclusion in the next edition of Marine Corps Reference Publication (MCRP) 5-12C, *Marine Corps Supplement to the Department of Defense Dictionary of Military and Associated Terms.*

Throughout this publication, the HRST master's commands are in bold italic text. All other commands are in italic text.

Personnel

A safe HRST evolution is the responsibility of all participants, from the unit commander to the individual roper. To ensure a safe training evolution and to provide a dynamic environment for HRST operations, a clear understanding of the responsibilities of all those involved is required. This chapter tasks and defines specific responsibilities associated with HRST operations.

Unit Commander

A unit commander's primary responsibility is to ensure that all HRST is accomplished in a safe manner and in accordance with this publication and Marine Corps Order (MCO) 3500.42, *Marine Corps HRST Policy and Program Administration.* Additional responsibilities include, but are not limited to, the following:

- Ensuring that HRST within the unit is conducted and supervised by an HRST master and safety insert officer (SIO) who are certified and current in accordance with MCO 3500.42.
- Ensuring that all HRST certifications and currency dates are properly recorded (i.e., in a service record book, officer qualification record, and/or training record) in accordance with MCO 3500.42.
- Ensuring that all personnel conducting HRST from a helicopter have successfully completed static tower training within the parameters established in MCO 3500.42.
- Ensuring that all HRST equipment assigned on the unit's table of equipment is properly maintained, inspected, and stowed after use.

HRST Master

The HRST master's primary responsibility is the overall safety of all ropers and the conduct and safety of the HRST operation. Therefore, the HRST master must know and understand this publication and all current HRST policies and directives. Once planning begins, the HRST master oversees safety and continues to monitor safety throughout the entire HRST evolution. HRST equipment serviceability and safety is also the responsibility of the HRST master (see chap. 2).

Descent and extraction authority is the sole responsibility of the HRST master. However, the aircraft commander may abort or cancel a descent/extraction if conditions are considered unsafe. During special patrol insertion and extraction (SPIE), the HRST master informs the aircraft commander when the ropers are connected and ready to lift. The crew chief checks for obstacles and clears the aircraft commander for lift and transition to forward flight. During fast roping and rappelling, the HRST master is responsible for the precise placement of the rope on the target area. If safe conditions for descent are not met, the HRST master ceases the operation.

If the mission dictates, the HRST master may participate as a roper. If participating as a roper, the HRST master is the last man out. If the HRST master is not required to participate as a roper, he remains on board the helicopter.

HRST master responsibilities include—

Preflight
- Conducting a detailed briefing of all personnel to be inserted/extracted (see app. A for an example of a mission brief).
- Conducting a face-to-face brief with the aircrew (see app. B for an example of a brief to an aircrew).
- Ensuring that HRST commands (see app. C) and emergency procedures are clearly understood by all participants.
- Ensuring proper attachment, installation, padding, and inspection of all ropes and devices associated with the HRST.
- Inspecting the floor surface of the aircraft and notifying the aircrew if any fluid spills are found on the helicopter's floor.
- Ensuring that a machete and a cutting block are available for use during emergencies.

In-flight
- Maintaining a line of communications with the aircrew at all times; either by an internal communications system (ICS) or the use of hand-and-arm signals if the ICS fails.
- Responding (challenge and reply) to all voice commands from the aircraft commander.
- Complying with all aircrew instructions.
- Deploying the rope or directing it to be deployed only after the helicopter has been stabilized in a hover and the aircraft commander commands, "*Deploy the rope.*"
- Ensuring the orderly movement of ropers from their strapped-in position to the rope station.

- Performing a final inspection of ropers as they approach the rope station (checking for loose equipment or missing safety gear).
- Monitoring the ropers' descent until they are safely clear of the rope and advising the aircrew of any problems.
- Monitoring the condition and security of the rope and anchor points, being watchful for signs of wear and slippage.
- Ensuring that ropes maintain proper contact with the ground and advising the aircrew when proper contact is not maintained.
- Retrieving or releasing the rope once all ropers are safely on the deck and clear of the deplaning station.
- Cutting the rope only in case of an emergency and only after the aircraft commander commands, "*Cut rope.*"

Post flight
- Derigging all HRST equipment and padding from the helicopter.
- Conducting a post flight debrief with all HRST participants.
- Inspecting all HRST equipment for wear and stowing all equipment properly (see chap. 2).
- Making appropriate log book rope usage entries.

Safety Insert Officer

The SIO will be a current HRST master since he has overall responsibility for the HRST, which includes ensuring the safety of overseeing and supervising all phases of the HRST. Therefore, the SIO must know and understand this publication and all current HRST policies and directives.

The SIO will be present for every phase of training. Whenever possible, the SIO is located in the drop zone and uses radio communications to monitor the safety of the operation. If the SIO cannot be in the drop zone, he will be in the helicopter and the first roper on the deck.

The SIO's supervisory responsibilities include, but are not limited to, the following:

- Ensuring that all HRST master's briefs are conducted.
- Ensuring that the aircraft commander briefs conduct of the flight and emergency procedures.
- Completing pre-operation/post operation inspections of helicopter rigging and equipment.
- Ensuring that the aircrew has all required aviation equipment and that the equipment is used properly by HRST personnel (e.g., ICS headset and gunner's belt for the HRST master).
- Monitoring the helicopter radio frequency being used and being prepared to issue warnings and instructions.
- Issuing the "*Abort*" command any time the HRST training is not proceeding as briefed, the aircrew is having difficulty in maintaining a steady hover, or in the event of any other unforeseen circumstance that may impact safety.

Aircraft Commander

The aircraft commander's primary responsibility is the safe conduct of the flight. Specific responsibilities are as follows:

Preflight

- Performing detailed preflight planning to ensure there is sufficient helicopter power, and that the weather, ambient light, and drop zone conditions are conducive to safe HRST operations.
- Ensuring that helicopter floor surfaces to be used for HRST are clean, dry, and free of oily substances.
- Inspecting HRST rigging to ensure that it is adequately padded and that it will not damage the helicopter or create a hazard.
- Conducting a thorough face-to-face brief with the HRST master and SIO. The brief shall include—
  - o Conduct of the flight.
  - o Hover altitude.
  - o Number of ropers.
  - o Communications procedures between aircrew, HRST master, and SIO (to include procedures if electronic communications fail).

- o Aircraft commander, HRST master, and crew chief responsibilities.
- o HRST personnel responsibilities in the event of a helicopter emergency.

In-flight

- Conducting the flight as briefed.
- Authorizing "*Deploy the rope*" once established in a stable hover.
- Authorizing "*Abort*" the mission if helicopter or environmental factors prohibit a stable hover.
- Ensuring that a line of communications is maintained between aircrew, HRST master, and SIO.
- Responding (challenge and reply) to all commands from the crew chief and HRST master.
- Authorizing "*Cut rope*" in the event of a helicopter emergency and no other options are available.

Note: The aircraft commander has sole responsibility to order that a rope be cut. Cutting a rope is the last alternative and only used in an effort to save lives.

Post flight

- Participating in a thorough debrief of all HRST members.

Crew Chief

The crew chief's primary responsibility during HRST is to assist the pilot with terrain/obstacle clearance and to assist with maintaining the helicopter over the target area by passing voice instructions to the pilot. During HRST, the crew chief assumes certain responsibilities and duties in addition to his normal aircrew member duties:

Preflight

- Ensures that operable ICS headsets and gunner's belts are available for the HRST master and his assistants, as required.
- Ensures that helicopter floor surfaces used for HRST are clean, dry, and free of oily substances.

- Installs the Schlomer frame, fast rope gantry, fast rope anchor bar, or A-frame fast rope attachment bar as required.
- Ensures that loose equipment and rope ends do not create hazards or preclude movement inside the helicopter.
- Participates in the preflight HRST brief to the aircrew and, when possible, attends the HRST mission brief to HRST members.

In-flight

- Assists the pilot in maintaining a steady hover by passing voice instructions concerning the helicopter's position over the target area.
- Assists the HRST master in passing voice instructions to the aircraft commander in the event of ICS failure.
- Ensures that all HRST masters wear gunner's belts when operating in the vicinity of a rope station.
- Ensures that all ropers remain strapped in until instructed to "*Unbuckle*" by the HRST master.
- Monitors the condition and security of ropes and anchor points, being watchful for signs of wear and slippage.
- Ensures that all ropes are clear of ropers and that all ropes are either retrieved, released, or clear of ground obstacles before passing clearance for forward flight to the aircraft commander.
- Advises that the helicopter is clear for forward flight by passing "*Clear for forward flight*" to the aircraft commander.

Post flight

- Participates in the post flight debrief of all HRST members
- Ensures that HRST equipment has been properly removed from the helicopter.

Crew Coordination

Crew coordination is critical to safe HRST operations. Coordination involves informational briefings, effective and responsive communications, and an understanding of HRST commands.

Briefings

Face-to-face briefings involve all HRST participants. The HRST master gives a detailed HRST mission brief to HRST participants (see app. A). If possible, the aircrew should be present during the HRST mission brief to HRST participants.

The HRST brief to the aircrew (see app. B) is conducted by the HRST master and the SIO. The aircraft commander briefs emergency procedures to all HRST participants.

Communications and HRST Commands

Internal Communications System

An operable ICS is mandatory for HRST. ICS headsets must be provided for all HRST masters. Loud and clear intercommunications among the pilots, the crew chief, and the HRST master must be maintained at all times. In the event of ICS failure, hand-and-arm signals are used to cease training until an operable ICS can be restored.

Challenge and Reply

The method of challenge and reply is mandatory for all HRST commands between the aircrew and the HRST master. Challenge and reply provides clarity to intercommunications and assurance to all HRST participants that commands have been passed and received.

Radio Communications

Operable radio communications must be maintained between the helicopter and the SIO, who is located in the drop zone. If the SIO is aboard the helicopter, he uses the ICS.

Hand-and-arm Signals

Ropers must rely on hand-and-arm signals and verbal commands from the HRST master for communications. Therefore, a clear understanding of all HRST commands and hand-and-arm signals is mandatory by all HRST participants and aircrew (see app. C).

Safety

It is each Marine's responsibility to understand and comply with the information in this publication so that a safe training environment is maintained. Every Marine involved in HRST has the authority to question an unsafe situation and to have any unsafe situation corrected prior to the continuation of training. Only personnel qualified in accordance with MCO 3500.42 can conduct HRST operations. The following factors affect HRST operations. These measures are minimum safety requirements and must be complied with.

Environmental Factors

Environmental factors may affect the aircraft commander's ability to safely maintain the position of the helicopter over the target area. Also, the effects of altitude, temperature, and humidity greatly affect helicopter performance. The following precautions must be taken to mitigate the effects of environmental factors:

- A minimum of 10 feet vertical clearance and 15 feet horizontal clearance from obstacles are mandatory while conducting a hover for HRST operations.
- Care must be taken to select a drop/pickup zone that is relatively free of dust, snow, or other objects that could obscure the aircraft commander's vision.
- HRST operations must be aborted if the aircraft commander is unable to detect a visible horizon or acquire visual reference points due to weather conditions (e.g., fog, haze) or other factors.
- The aircraft commander must complete a proper weight and balance calculation to determine if environmental factors permit safe HRST operations.

Night Factors

Night operations can affect an aircraft commander's ability to maintain a steady position over the target area. They also challenge the HRST master's ability to maintain control of ropers during the conduct of HRST. During nighttime operations, the aircrew wears night vision devices (NVDs) as directed by current policy.

Helicopter Factors

The following precautions enhance safety inside the helicopter:

- Loose combat gear, padding, and rope ends that can create a tripping hazard to ropers as they move to their rope stations must be secured inside the helicopter.
- When HRST operations involve descending through the hell hole, all personnel inside the helicopter must be particularly cautious to avoid accidentally falling through the hell hole. Whenever possible the hatch to the hell hole remains closed until required for use.
- A qualified HRST master will be located at each rope station to ensure safety.

In addition to safety considerations inside the helicopter, personnel must also be aware of the following safety issues.

Rotor Downwash

Participants must be aware of the following effects of rotor downwash:

- Rotor downwash pushes ropers down the rope; therefore ropers must be prepared to apply additional braking.
- Rotor downwash causes sand and small objects to be blown into the drop/pickup zone. Ropers must wear approved eye protection goggles to

avoid eye injury from flying debris. Long-sleeve clothing is also required to avoid cuts, abrasions, and skin irritations.

- The size of the helicopter affects the rotor downwash (large helicopters have greater rotor downwash than small helicopters).
- The weight of the helicopter increases the rotor downwash effect (the more weight the greater the rotor downwash).

See figure 1-1.

Hover Height

Hover height is affected by numerous factors; therefore, a specific altitude cannot be established for all HRST operations. The following examples impact hover height:

- Rotor downwash can agitate a rope hanging from the helicopter and cause the rope to whip, creating a dangerous situation. A slightly higher hover reduces the effect of rotor downwash on the ground and the rope.
- During wooded or mountain area HRST operations, hover heights are restricted to the lowest possible height commensurate with rope length, obstacle clearance, visual cues, soil stability, and rotor downwash.

Static Discharge

Static electricity is generated by a helicopter and is discharged from the aircraft by contact with the ground. Therefore, personnel will not be in con-

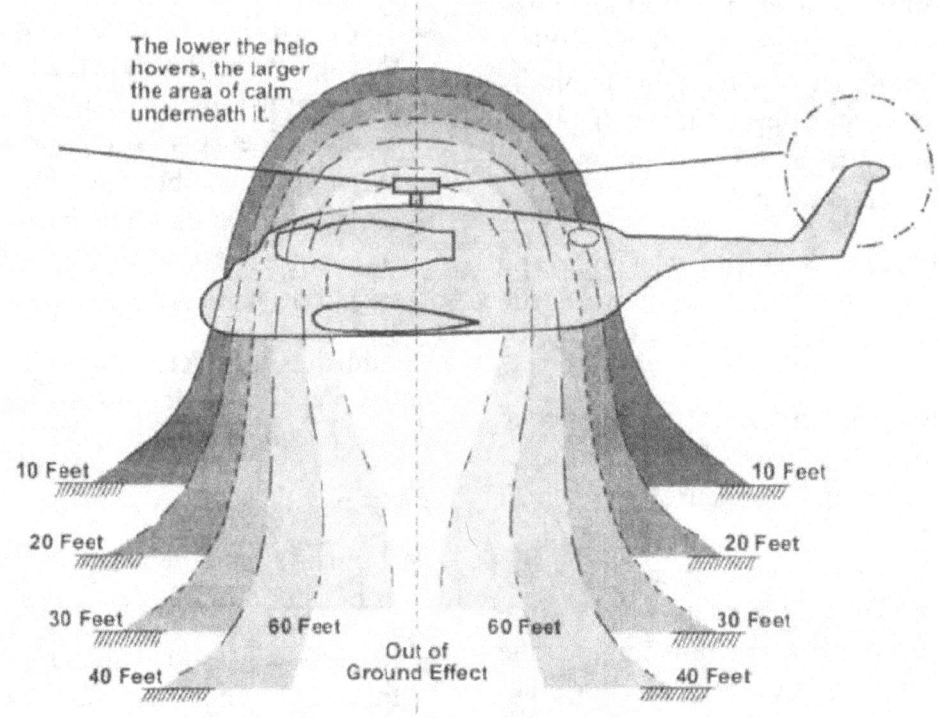

Legend:

~~~~~~~~ Ground surface

Shaded areas are the zones of calm air beneath a helicopter hovering at different heights. This chart compares the relatively calm areas underneath a helicopter hovering at four different heights. If you start at the pair of marks that designate 40 feet, you'll see that the calm areas get wider as the helicopter gets lower.

Figure 1-1. Rotor Downwash.

tact with the rope as it touches the ground due to the possibility that the rope may conduct static electricity. HRST operations will not commence until the rope has made contact with the ground.

Dry ropes are nonconductive and do not allow static electricity to be discharged through them. However, ropers may experience a small harmless shock upon reaching the ground due to the body's ability to conduct an electrical charge. Ropes may become conductive if they are wet.

Equipment and Clothing Safety

Padding

The entire edge of the ramp, door, or hatch across which a rope is expected to lie or rub, is covered with appropriate material (e.g., fire hose, carpet, or other suitable material) to ensure that all sharp edges are padded. Taping over the edges is not acceptable; edges must be both padded and taped. Surfaces must be clean and free of oily fluids so that tape will adhere and padding can be adequately secured.

Safety Ropes/Anchor Points

Whenever possible, HRST operations are conducted with a redundancy of safety backup ropes and rope anchor points:

- Ensure that the weight on the rope is evenly spread-loaded to numerous anchor points.
- Incorporate secondary and tertiary anchor points in all rope configurations.

Clothing

Marines should avoid wearing loose, bulky clothing in order to reduce the possibility of clothing snagging on protruding objects or becoming fouled in ropes. The following safety clothing is a minimum requirement to ensure personnel safety:

- The utility uniform is worn: sleeves rolled down and buttoned, blouse tucked into the trousers, belt buckle moved to the left hand side.
- HRST participants wear appropriate head protection according to mission requirements.
- HRST participants wear appropriate eye protection according to mission requirements.
- A heavy leather outer glove and a lighter material liner are required for rappelling and fast rope operations.
- Earplugs or other sound suppressive devices are required for helicopter operations.
- A 12 to 15 foot piece of rappelling rope is used to create a military rappel seat or safety harness.
- A life preserver personal (LPP) or other approved personal flotation device (PFD) and an approved emergency escape breathing device is mandatory for HRST operations over water.
- A gunner's belt (see fig. 1-2) is mandatory for the HRST master or any HRST participant who is positioned at a helicopter opening or rope station. To enhance the effectiveness of the belt in the event of an emergency, it should be worn above the waist as high as possible (i.e., under the armpits). The gunner's belt must allow the HRST master to reach the rope station.

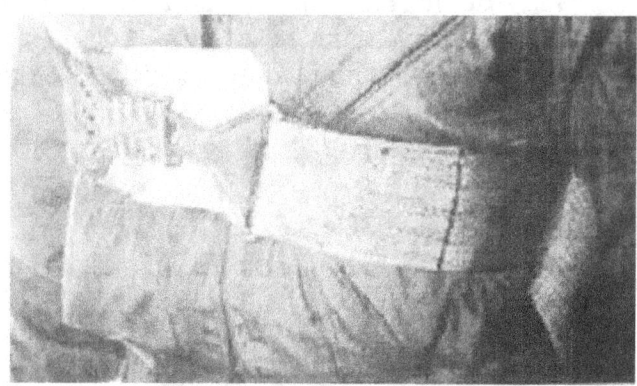

Figure 1-2. Gunner's Belt.

Figure 1-3. Position of Weapon

Figure 1-4. Position of Equipment.

- Operational equipment, when required, is placed to reduce the possibility of snagging:
  - o Weapons are worn with the muzzle pointed down and away from the brake hand while rappelling (see fig. 1-3). The rifle is attached by 550 cord, rifle sling, or similar material.
  - o When combat gear is worn, the cartridge belt may be buckled behind the roper to keep equipment clear during a fast rope descent. If buckled in the front, equipment should be removed from the right hand side of the cartridge belt during rappelling operations.
  - o When a pack is worn, combat gear may be placed inside of the pack. If combat gear is worn, equipment should be removed from the right hand side of the web belt (see fig. 1-4).

Accident Procedures

Medical personnel with the necessary medical equipment (i.e., backboard with straps, cervical collar, medical bag) and safety vehicle must be present during all HRST operations. In the event of an accident, the first priority is to injured personnel. If personnel are injured, they are transported to the closest military or civilian hospital. If possible, the nature of the injuries is radioed ahead and the aircraft/safety vehicle's estimated time of arrival. Once injured personnel are stabilized, the proper authorities are notified, statements obtained from witnesses, and appropriate reports filed.

CHAPTER 2
ROPES, EQUIPMENT, AND KNOTS

The safety of all ropers depends upon the condition and serviceability of HRST equipment. Therefore, ground and aviation maintenance personnel must ensure that damaged and unserviceable equipment is not used.

The ropes, equipment, and knots discussed in this chapter are approved for HRST operations. Deviations or substitutions must be approved through the appropriate chain of command to the Commandant of the Marine Corps, Deputy Commandant, Plans, Policies and Operations (CMC, DC, PP&O).

Ground Equipment

The equipment discussed in this paragraph is provided and maintained by the ground unit conducting the HRST.

Rope Management

A new rope is physically inspected for any signs of damage or defects. After passing inspection, both ends of the rappel rope are burnt. The free end of a fast rope is not burnt but whipped with 550 cord (see fig. 2-1).

All ropes are checked for wear, cuts, frays, burns, mildew, and rotten areas both before and after every use. All ropes used in HRST must be free of splices.

The unit stores and maintains all HRST ropes in a clean, well-ventilated, dry area. If a rope becomes soiled, shake it clean or rinse it with fresh water and lay it out to dry before storage. If a rope becomes wet, either in storage or during use, dry it as soon as possible. To dry a rope, uncoil it and lay it in a well-ventilated area. If possible, suspend the rope off the deck, on wooden pegs, or

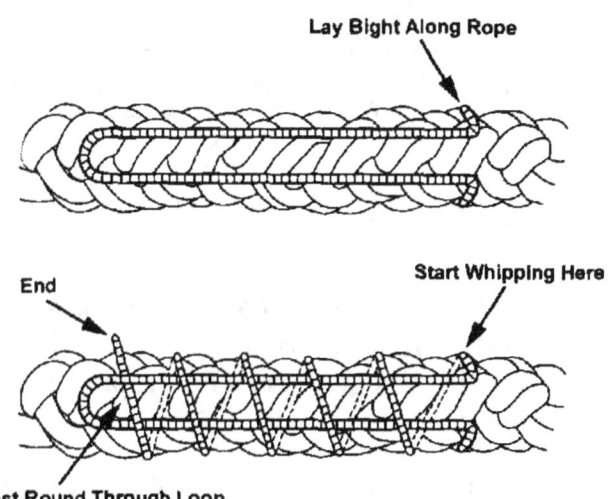

Figure 2-1. Whipping End of the Fast Rope.

on a rack to reduce drying time. If any part of a rope comes in contact with any type of petroleum products (e.g., fuel, oil) the rope is considered unserviceable as a lifeline and is removed from service. If a fast rope comes in contact with salt water rinse it with fresh water and clean with a nonmetallic brush.

A record of each rappel rope's use and condition is maintained in a rope log (see app. D).

Never keep a rope knotted or stretched longer than necessary because it stretches and weakens the rope. Never stand, walk, or step on a rope or smoke within 50 feet of a rope, all these can weaken the rope. Protect nylon rope and webbing from direct sunlight as much as possible to avoid ultraviolet deterioration.

Grading a Rope

Ropes are graded based on their usage and appearance. Using the criteria established in table 2-1 (on page 2-2) rope serviceability can be determined. Ropes that do not meet the criteria established in table 2-1 are classified as unserviceable. Rappel

Table 2-1. Rope Grading,

Grade	Definition	Appearance	Use
I	A new rappel line not older than 2 years with no more than 500 rappels on it.	Little or no wear.	High/low rappel towers of 100 feet or less and combat equipped rappels or helicopter rappels.
II	A rappel line older than 2 years with 500 but less than 1,000 rappels on it.	Shows slight external wear. Furry on outer sheath.	High/low rappel towers of 100 feet or less. No combat equipment stress exposure.
III	A rappel line with more than 5 years or 1,000 rappels.	Shows slight external wear. Furry on outer sheath.	Sling ropes and rappel seats.

ropes have a shelf life of 7 years and a service life of 5 years. SPIE ropes have a shelf life of 15 years and a service life of 7 years. Fast ropes have neither a shelf nor a service life.

Proper periodic inspections of the rappel ropes are conducted throughout the rappel operation: every 30 minutes or 50 rappels. Whenever hourglass indentations, burns, excessive sheath wear, cuts to sheath, or visible stress/elongations are detected, the rope is removed from service. Contact with petroleum, oils, and lubricants (POLs) or petroleum-based solvents also permanently deadline a rappel rope. Ropes will not be authorized for further use within the rope grading table matrix if any of this criteria is found.

A grade III rope is a rope that is nearing its deadline limits, either through visual inspection or usage. Sling ropes and rappel seats may be cut from the points in the rope that are not excessively worn. However, these sections must meet the same frequent visual safety inspections for hourglass indentations, burns, excessive sheath wear, cuts to sheath, or visible stress/elongation. Because the sling rope may be used as a rappel seat, it is necessary to maintain a high inspection awareness. Use of a worn sling rope for a rappel seat can be catastrophic, because unlike rappel lines used in tandem, the sling rope has no secondary back-up upon failure.

SPIE and fast ropes grading emphasizes a visual inspection for serviceability. Visual inspections for both fast ropes and SPIE ropes are as follows:

SPIE rope
- Check for excessive abrasion, fraying, or one complete, broken strand.
- Inspect D-ring attachment points for corrosion and cracks.

Fast rope
- Burns.
- Cuts.
- Abraded yarns.
- Loose braiding.
- Strand kinking.
- Loose or missing whipping.

Although fast ropes and SPIE ropes gradually change color, these color changes do not indicate a decrease in strength unless the change is due to contact with strong chemicals. If a rope has had chemical contact, its color change will not be uniform throughout the length of the rope.

Removing a Rope From Service

Any rope that is considered defective or unserviceable is removed from service and tagged with the nature of the defect, the cause, and the date of inspection. The tag is signed by an HRST master. Any HRST master has the authority to remove any rope from service that he determines to be defective or unserviceable.

Coiling a Rope

All HRST ropes should be coiled when not in use and hung from a wooden peg or cylindrical object. Ropes will not be hung on any type of metal or steel object because of the possibility of rust. When coiling a rope, avoid knots and entanglements and provide maximum ventilation to the rope surface. Place SPIE and fast ropes in parachute kit bags for protection when not in use. There are two types of coils for rappel ropes: mountain coil and butterfly coil.

Mountain Coil

The mountain coil is the least preferred method of coiling a rope because the rope tends to tangle up during uncoiling (see fig. 2-2).

Butterfly Coil

The butterfly coil is the most preferred method of coiling because it tangles less and can be tied across the back (see fig. 2-3).

Rope and SPIE Equipment Stowage

To stow ropes and SPIE equipment, ensure the following:

- Ropes and equipment are at least 4 inches from walls when stored on shelves.
- Ropes and equipment are at least 4 inches from the floor when stored in bins.
- Storage areas are well ventilated and free from oil, acid, cleaning compounds, and other contaminants.
- Ropes and equipment are not stowed above or near hot water pipes, heating apparatuses, or direct sun light.

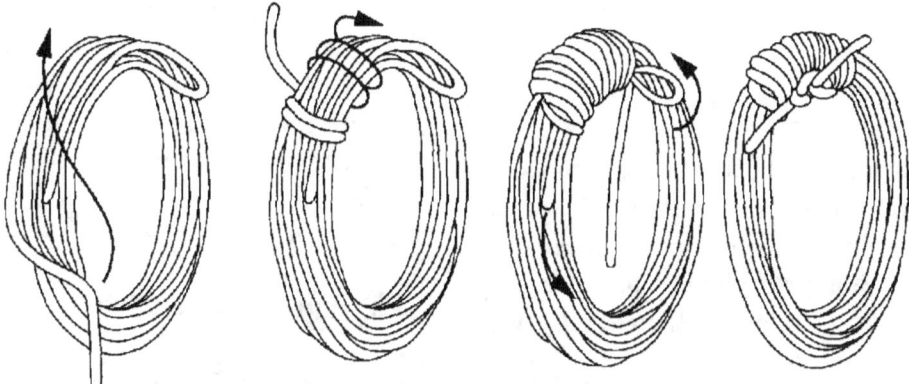

Figure 2-2. Mountain Coil.

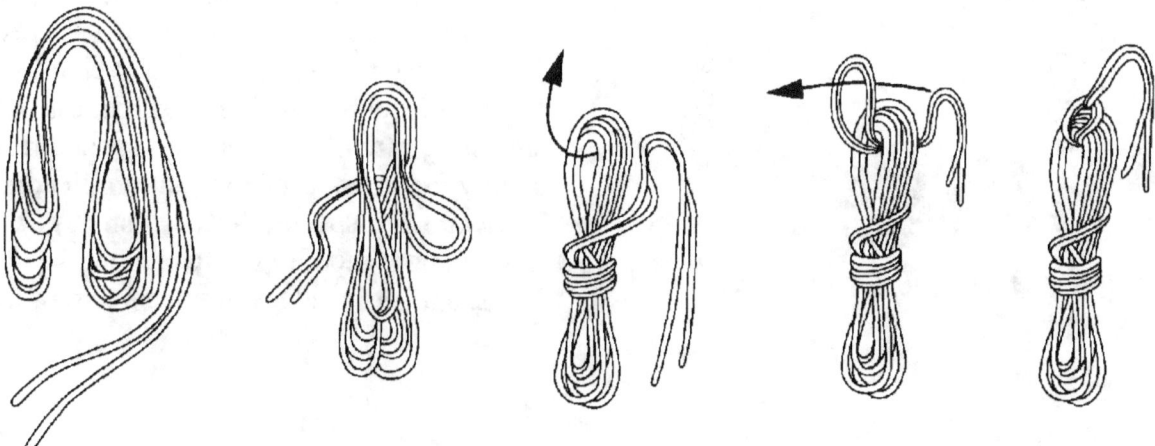

Figure 2-3. Butterfly Coil.

Static Kernmantle Rope

General service contract #: GS07F14181

Diameter: 11mm

Tensile strength: 6,500 lbs

Length: Commonly 150 ft, available up to 600 ft spool

Color: Olive drab/black

The static kernmantle rope consists of a high strength inner core that is covered by an outer woven sheath.

Plimoore Fast Rope

Part number: 30 ft—3336681 (used as a training device at MCRD San Diego/Parris Island, no NSN assigned)

NSN: 60 ft—4020-01-500-5765
      90 ft— 4020-01-500-5766
      120 ft—4020-01-500-5779

Fast rope diameter: 1¾ in

Fast rope tensile strength: 35,000 lbs

The plimoore fast rope is military green in color and consists of multiple strands with a right-hand lay weave. It is made of multifilament polyester over multifilament polypropylene. The rope has an end cap assembly with a 3-inch steel ring for aircraft anchoring. See figure 2-4.

Figure 2-4. Plimoore Fast Rope.

SPIE Rope

NSN: 120 ft white rope—1670-01-065-0851
        120 ft black rope—1670-01-501-5491

D-ring: part number 101407

Diameter: 1 in

Tensile strength: 24,000 lbs
               D-rings—5,000 lbs

The SPIE rope assembly consists of two tapered eye splices, one at each end. The tapered eye splice, used for attaching the rope to the helicopter, is encapsulated in polyurethane for protection from abrasion. The rope itself is coated with a nylon solution that protects the core of the rope. There are five pairs of D-rings that start 7 feet from the running end of the rope, are spaced 1 foot apart, and are 7 feet from the center to the center of the succeeding pair of rings. See figure 2-5.

The SPIE system is inspected by a qualified HRST master at 6 month intervals and when serviceability is questioned. All inspections are documented in the rope log book. Using units will comply with service life limitations contained in NAVAIR 13-45-2, *Special Patrol Insertion/ Extraction (SPIE) System.*

SPIE Harness Assembly

NSN: 1670-01-068-8342

Inspect harness and suspension sling webbing for signs of contamination from oil, grease, acid, and rust. Inspect for signs of wear such as cuts, twists, fading, fusing, fraying, burns, abrasions, and loose or broken stitches. A damaged harness or suspension sling is removed from service and returned to supply for appropriate disposition. In addition, all hardware is inspected for corrosion, pitting, ease of operation, security of attachment, bends, dents, nicks, and sharp edges. Replacement of hardware

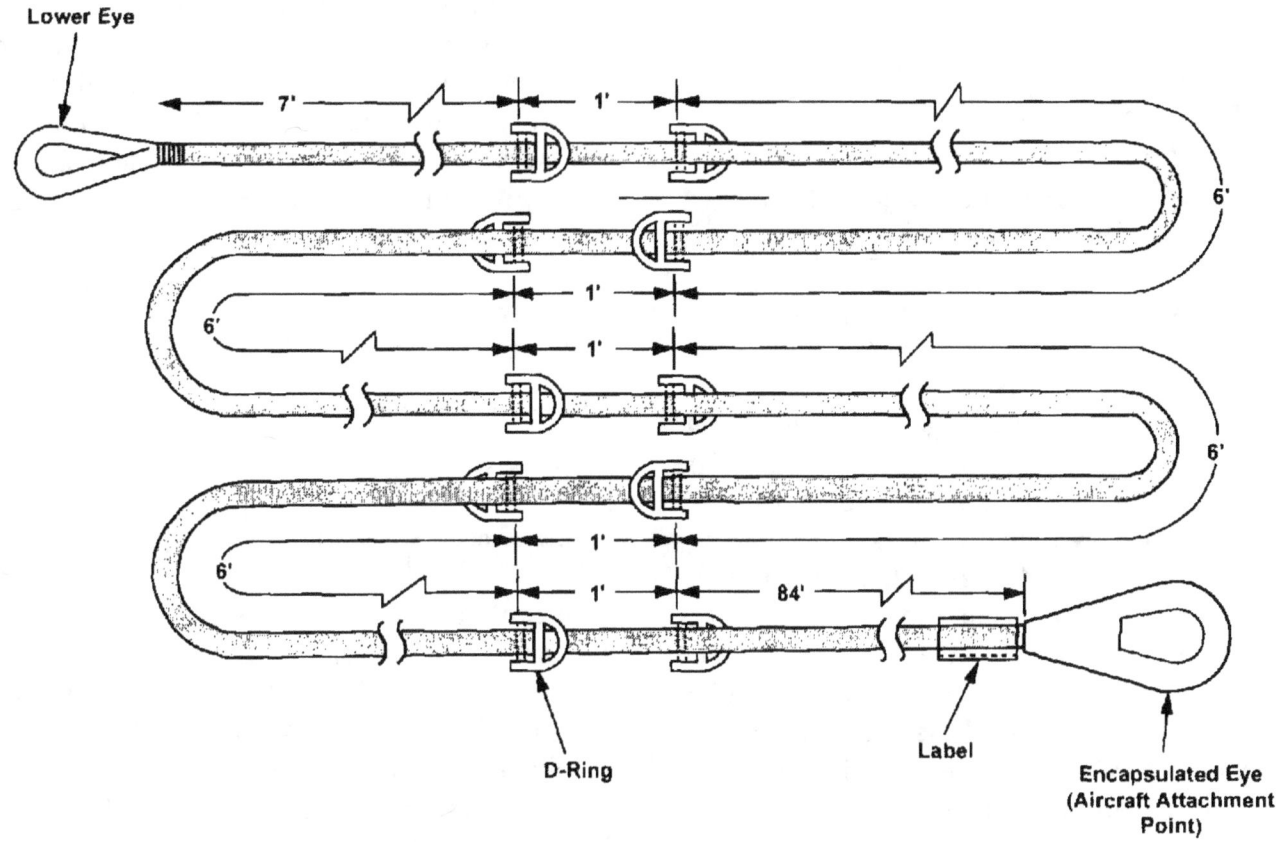

Lower Eye

7'

1'

6'

6'

1'

1'

6'

6'

1'

1'

84'

D-Ring

Label

Encapsulated Eye
(Aircraft Attachment
Point)

Figure 2-5. SPIE Rope.

that requires unstitching or cutting of webbing renders the entire harness, except chest strap adapter, unserviceable. If damaged, the harness suspension sling is returned to supply for appropriate disposition. The SPIE harness consists of basic nylon fabric with two leg straps and a chest strap (see fig. 2-6). The leg straps connect around the Marine's legs with an ejector/quick release snap that snaps into adjustable V-rings. The chest strap laces through the buckle and is then back laced for a quick release. On the back of the harness is a reversible (left or right) pick up strap into which a steel locking carabiner is inserted for attachment of the harness to the SPIE rope.

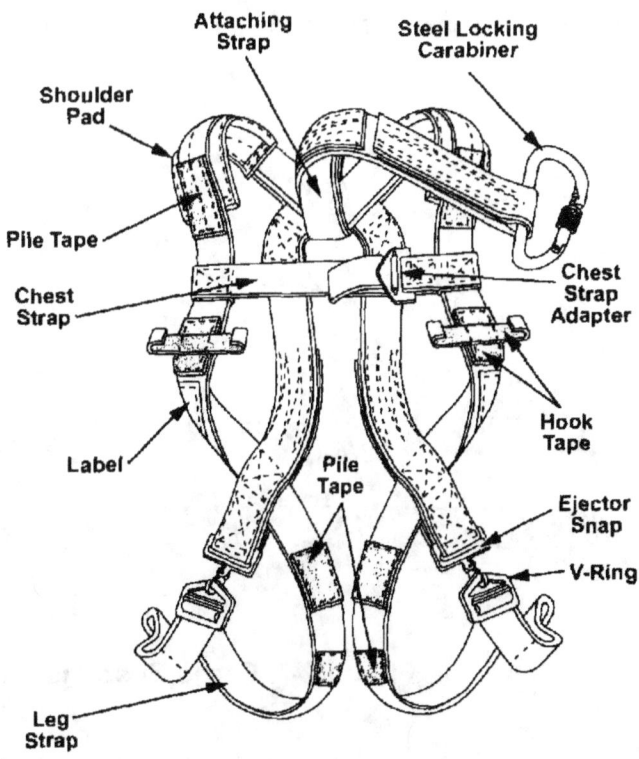

Attaching
Strap

Steel Locking
Carabiner

Shoulder
Pad

Pile Tape

Chest
Strap
Adapter

Chest
Strap

Hook
Tape

Label

Pile
Tape

Ejector
Snap

V-Ring

Leg
Strap

Figure 2-6. SPIE Harness.

Cargo Suspension Sling with Type IV Connector

NSN: Slings—2350-09-000-0918
Type IV connector—1670-00-783-5988

Tensile strengths: Type-26, multi-loop sling—14,000 lbs
Type IV connector—40,000 lbs

The type-26, multi-loop, cargo suspension sling comes in multiple lengths; however, the 9-foot, two-loop, nylon sling is the only one authorized for SPIE operations. The cargo suspension slings are used as anchor points for the SPIE line. The type IV connector consists of a bottom plate assembly with two steel prongs and a spring-loaded top plate (see fig. 2-7). Inspection of the cargo suspension slings and type IV connector is done before and after each use. Inspect the sling for contamination from oil, grease, acid, or other foreign matter. Look for cuts, fraying, or burn marks on the webbing. The sling is unserviceable if more than three stitches in a row are loose or broken. Inspect the type IV connector for cracks, burrs, grooves, flaws, and rust. The top plate should be checked to ensure that the spring is functioning properly and that it locks the

retaining plate into place. Remove any rust with steel wool and apply a coating of a light non-petroleum based lubricant. Discard all type IV connectors that have two holes in the bottom plate assembly. Clean cargo suspension slings by scrubbing with a brush. Wet slings should be dried on a drying rack.

The cargo suspension sling service life is 7 years, and it has a shelf life of 15 years.

Stubai 85 Carabiner

NSN: 8465-01-276-8198

Tensile strength: 5,500 lbs

The Stubai 85 carabiner is a D-shaped, steel, modified, locking carabiner with a locking nut (see fig. 2-8). The Stubai 85 carabiner is used for all HRST systems. It is difficult to record the number of rappels executed on a carabiner; therefore, frequent inspection is required. Inspect the Stubai 85 carabiner for burrs and rust. Inspect the locking gate spring to ensure it closes and that the locking nut is secure. Discard unserviceable carabiners through appropriate supply channels after they have been marked with spray paint.

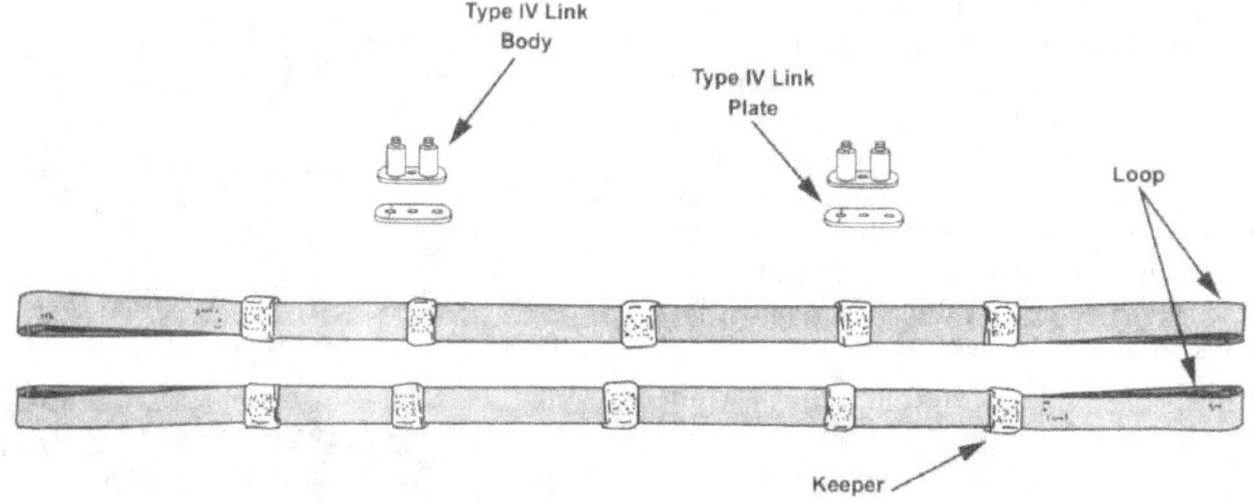

Figure 2-7. Cargo Suspension Sling with Type IV Connector.

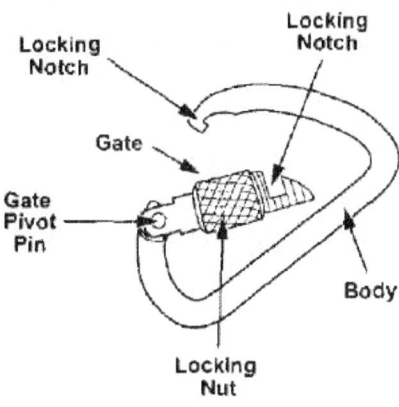

Figure 2-8. Stubai 85 Carabiner.

Omega 93 Carabiner

Model number: MD 716S3

Tensile strength: 8,818 lbs

The Omega 93 carabiner is a D-shaped, steel, modified, locking carabiner with a locking nut (see fig. 2-9). The Omega 93 carabiner is used for all HRST systems. It is difficult to record the number of rappels executed on a carabiner; therefore, frequent inspection is required. Inspect the Omega 93 carabiner for burrs and rust. Inspect the locking gate spring to ensure it closes and that the locking nut is secure. Discard unserviceable carabiners through appropriate supply channels after they have been marked with spray paint.

Figure 2-9. Omega 93 Carabiner.

10K Locking Carabiner

NSN: 4240-01-192-6272

Tensile strength: 10,000 lbs

The 10K locking carabiner is a steel, modified, D-shaped, locking carabiner with a locking nut (see fig. 2-10). The 10K carabiner is used for rigging the H-60 helicopter for HRST. Inspect the 10K carabiner for burrs and rust. Inspect the locking gate spring to ensure it closes and that the locking nut is secure. Discard unserviceable carabiners through appropriate supply channels after they have been marked with spray paint.

Figure 2-10. 10K Locking Carabiner.

G-12 Clevis

NSN: 4030-00-678-8562

Tensile strength: 20,000 lbs

The G-12 clevis is a ¾-inch shackle used to rig a braided eye fast rope to an H-60 helicopter's rescue hoist (see fig. 2-11).

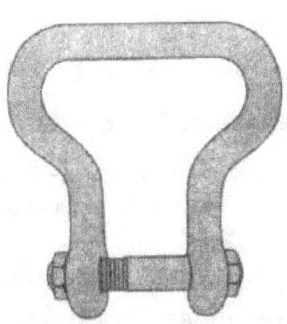

Figure 2-11. G-12 Clevis.

Rescue 8 Descender

| Tensile strength: Aluminum 7,000 lbs |
| Steel 40,000 lbs |

The Rescue 8 descender is a modified figure eight that is used when heavily-laden Marines are rappelling. The Rescue 8 has a set of ears extending out of the side that are used when tying off. The Rescue 8 descender is made out of either aluminum alloy or steel (see fig. 2-12).

Inspect the Rescue 8 descender for burrs or scratches that can cause cuts in the rope. The only effective method to detect structural flaws or cracks is through nondestructive inspection (NDI). NDI can be performed at a Marine Aviation Logistics Squadron (MALS) metal shop.

Figure 2-12. Rescue Descender.

Fast Rope Interface Kit

| ½-in double clevice connector (commonly called a James Walker) |
| NSN: Quick-release pins—5315-00-702-3139 |
| Steel locking carabiner—8465-01-276-8198 |
| Tensile strengths: Quick disconnect pins—2,950 lbs |
| Double clevice connector—9,200 lbs |

The fast rope interface kit consists of one, steel alloy double clevice assembly that incorporates one quick-release pin and one locking carabiner (see fig. 2-13). It is used to connect the fast rope to the primary anchor point for hell hole operations on the CH-46E helicopter.

Note: The ½-in double clevis connector (part number S-247-1/2) is a sole-source purchase item that can be ordered from the James Walker Company, 7109 Milford Industrial Rd, Pikesville, MD 21208, phone number (410) 486-3950.

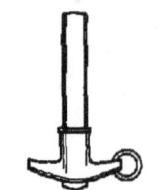

Quick-Release Pin

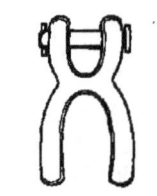

1/2" Double Clevice Connector

Steel Locking Carabiner

Figure 2-13. Fast Rope Interface Kit.

Leather Gloves

| NSN: 8415-00-634-4660 |

Rappel/fast rope personnel may use any heavy leather gloves approved by the HRST master. Heavy-duty, leather work gloves are consumable items, come in several styles, and may be purchased at self-service. However, welder's gloves are recommended for fast rope operations. Gauntlet gloves are not appropriate because the internal padding is positioned to protect the back of the hand and not the palm.

Sling Rope

A sling rope is a 12- to 15-foot piece of rappel rope that is 11mm in diameter and burnt on each end. It is used to construct military rappel seats and safety lines.

Tape

Military green, multi-use riggers or duct tape is used to protect ropes and lines at friction points on the helicopter and to secure fire hoses or other padding. Oil residues can seriously reduce the adhesive properties of the tape resulting in dislodgment of the protective system. Tape may be obtained through self-service.

Goggles

NSN: 8465-01-004-2893

Military impact plastic goggles with an elastic head strap are used to protect the eyes from sand and other flying debris.

Rigid Handle Machete

NSN: Machete—5110-00-813-1286
Sheath—8465-00-926-4932

The rigid handle machete is the only authorized emergency cutting device used for HRST operations. It is 18 inches long and 2 inches wide.

Rope Storage Bag

NSN: 8460-00-606-8366

The standard military parachutist kit bag is used for fast rope and SPIE rope storage.

Vario Sit Harness

NSN: 8465-01-415-5136

The vario sit harness is an alternative to the military rappel seat. It is made of nylon webbing and has an adjustable harness. Inspect harness and suspension sling webbing for signs of contamination from oil, grease, acid, and rust. Inspect for signs of wear such as cuts, twists, fading, fusing, fraying, burns, abrasions, and loose or broken stitches. A damaged harness or suspension sling is removed from service and returned to supply for appropriate disposition. In addition, inspect all hardware for corrosion, pitting, ease of operation, security of attachment, bends, dents, nicks, and sharp edges. Replacement of hardware that requires unstitching or cutting of webbing renders the entire harness, except chest strap adapter, unserviceable. If damaged, return the harness suspension sling to supply for appropriate disposition.

Jacob's Ladder

The Jacob's ladder is a 30- to 50-foot ladder that can be attached to the cargo tie down rings of a helicopter via three 2-inch eye splices. The ladder is deployed from the aircraft's ramp in order to extract personnel from areas where the helicopter could not otherwise land.

It can be purchased commercially or manufactured locally. When constructing the Jacob's ladder locally, the preferred method of construction is to use 11 millimeter static kermantle rope with wooden rungs. The rungs are cut in equal lengths and are attached to the rope through holes drilled in each end. When using rungs with holes drilled in the ends, knots must be placed above and below the rungs on the line to prevent the rungs from moving. It is important the rungs be placed perpendicular to the line. The rungs are then coated or wrapped with a non-skid type of material. Commerically available ladders must meet or exceed these standards.

Figure 2-14, on page 2-10, illustrates the typical construction of the Jacob's ladder. Ladders will vary in design depending on available materials and mission requirements.

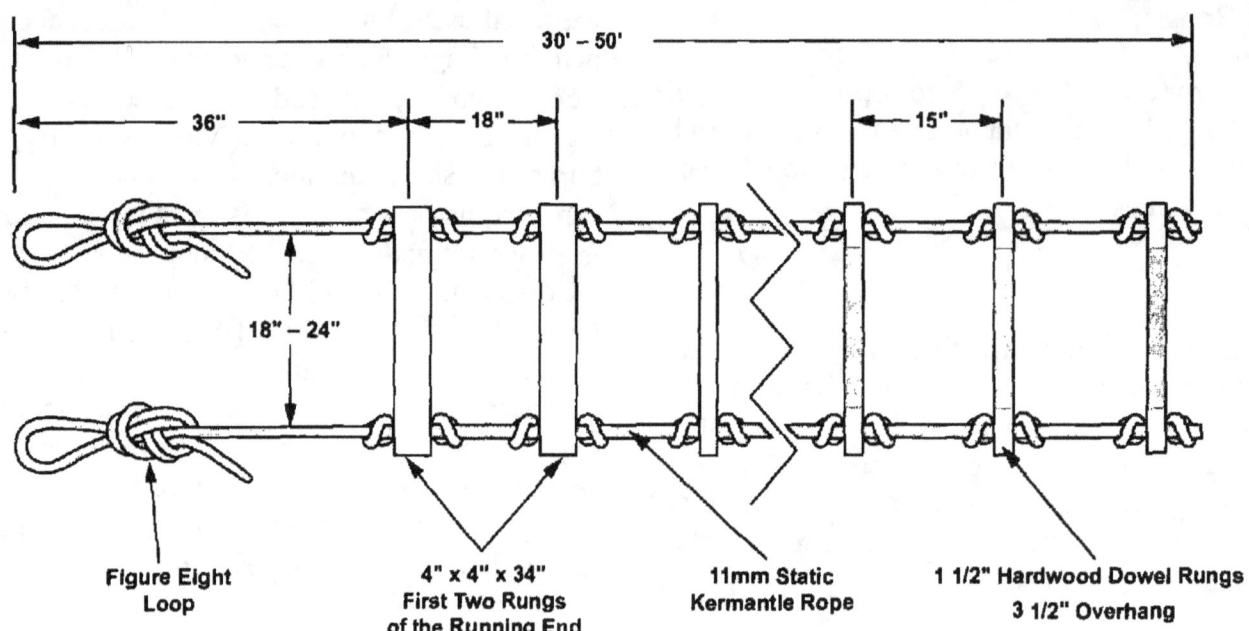

Figure 2-14. Jacob's Ladder Typical Construction (not to scale).

Aviation Equipment

The aviation unit supporting the HRST operation provides and maintains the following equipment.

Schlomer Frame

The Schlomer frame (see fig. 2-15) is used to attach one or two fast ropes at the ramp rope station of the CH-46E. It is manufactured at MALS and installed by the aircrew. It is a welded, tubular, collapsible steel frame (anchor points incorporate two quick-release pins that collapse the frame, allowing it to be stored when not in use). A serial number is etched and/or stamped on top of the frame above the quick-release pins.

The frame shall undergo NDI on a 365-day cycle. Repair and re-inspect any discrepancies or reject a frame that cannot be repaired. The frame is inspected for—

● Condition of all hardware (i.e., pins, cables).
● Condition of welds for cracks or fatigue.
● Condition of steel tubing for buckling, bending, rust, or deformation.
● Cracks, fatigue, and stress at all joints, welds, and stress point.

The Schlomer frame's usage is recorded on a Custody and Maintenance Record, which is maintained by the aircraft squadron.

Fast Rope Gantry

NSN: Boom rescue hoist—1680-00-120-0541

Base plate assembly: part number 205-072-236-1

The fast rope gantry is used to attach the fast rope at the forward cabin rope station on either side of the UH-1N helicopter (port or starboard). The fast rope gantry (see fig. 2-16 on page 2-12) is a pedestal and boom assembly that incorporates a base plate for mounting on the aircraft deck. It has a two-position locking arm for stowing or positioning for use. The fast rope gantry and base plate assembly are modified from the UH-1 rescue hoist boom. Once modified for fast rope use, the gantry is marked "FOR FAST ROPE ONLY." The fast rope gantry is installed by the aircrew.

The aircraft group maintains the gantry as an accountable piece of support equipment. The gantry's usage is recorded on a Custody and Maintenance Record.

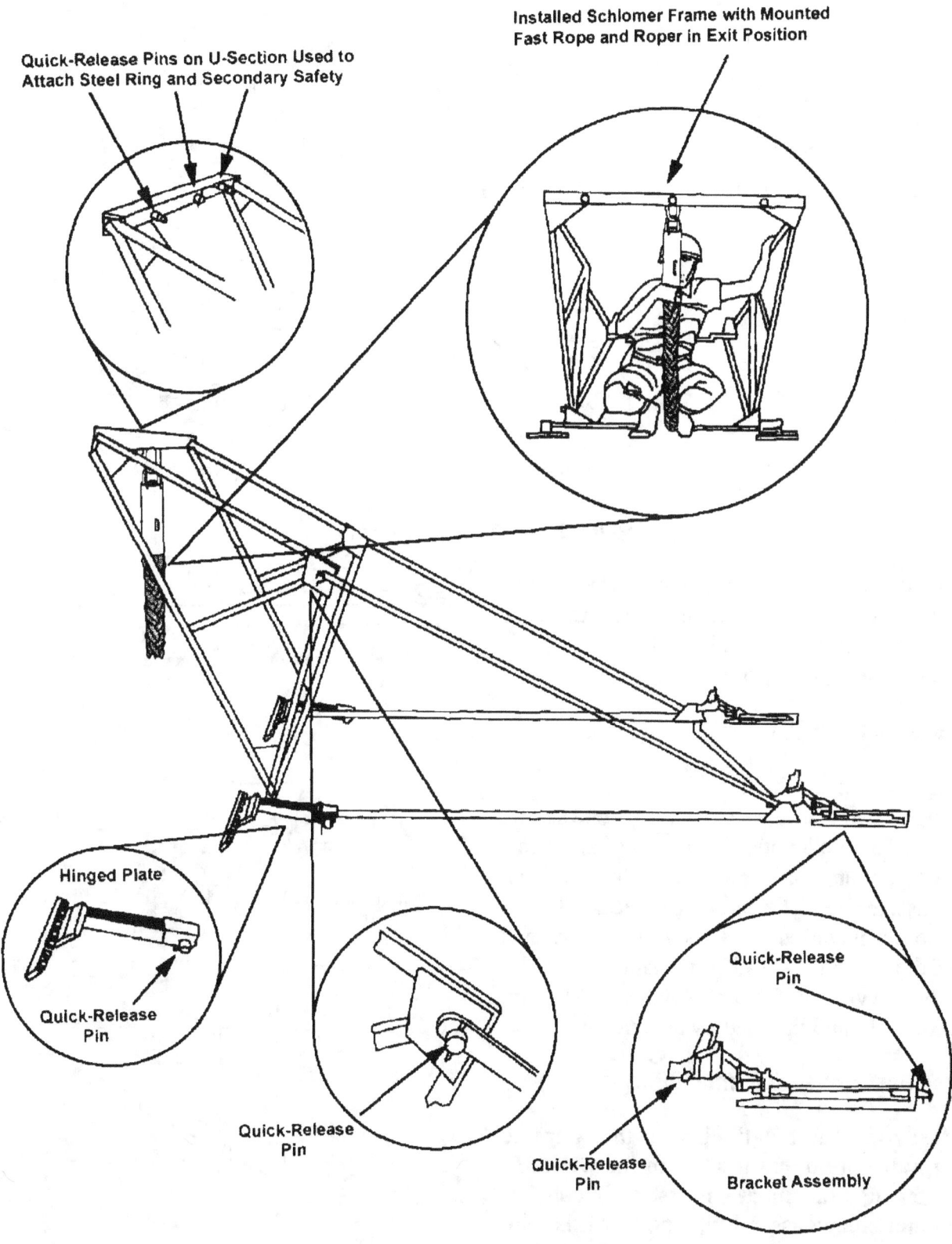

Quick-Release Pins on U-Section Used to
Attach Steel Ring and Secondary Safety

Installed Schlomer Frame with Mounted
Fast Rope and Roper in Exit Position

Hinged Plate

Quick-Release
Pin

Quick-Release
Pin

Quick-Release
Pin

Quick-Release
Pin

Bracket Assembly

Figure 2-15. Schlomer Frame.

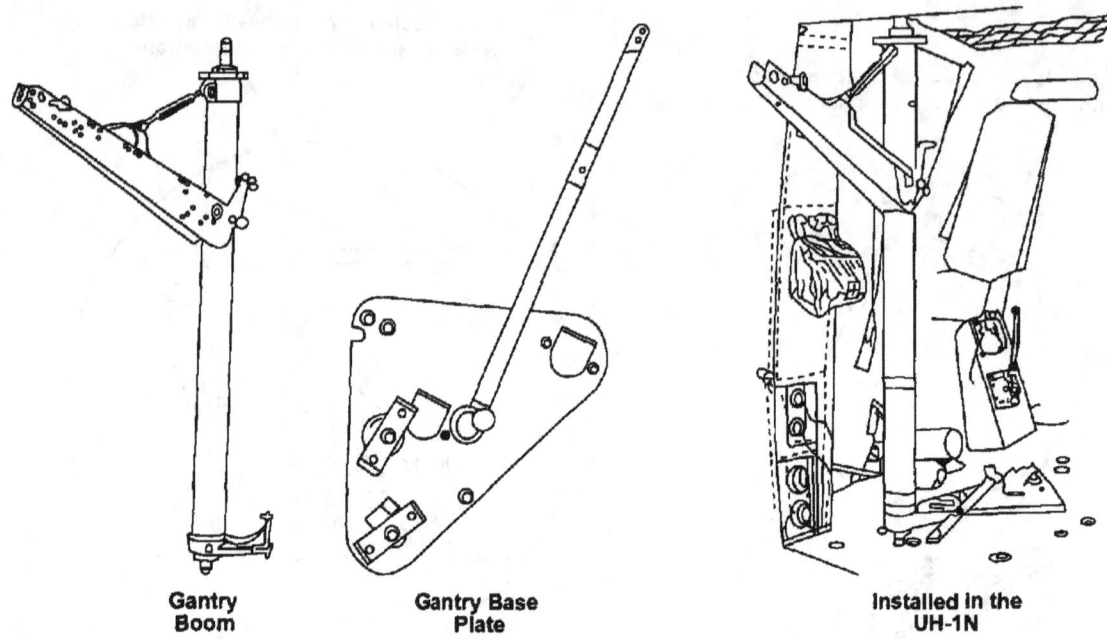

Gantry Boom	Gantry Base Plate	Installed in the UH-1N

Figure 2-16. Fast Rope Gantry.

Unless suspected of being damaged, inspection of the gantry follows the original maintenance inspection cycle established for the rescue hoist boom and base plate assembly.

Fast Rope Anchor Bar

The fast rope anchor bar (see fig. 2-17) is used to attach up to two fast ropes at the ramp rope station of the CH-53D helicopter. It consists of an aluminum alloy rectangular bar and two attached quick release assemblies. The anchor bar secures to two permanently installed brackets mounted on each side of the cabin bulkhead. It is manufactured by the Naval Aviation Depot, Naval Air Station, Pensacola, FL, and installed by the aircrew.

A-frame Fast Rope Attachment Bar Assembly

One fast rope can be attached to the A-frame during hell hole operations from the CH-53E. The A-frame attachment bar assembly consists of a monel sleeve assembly, a peanut link, and one 1-inch quick-release pin (see fig. 2-18). When installed, the bar replaces the two bolts used to attach the A-frame. It is manufactured by the MALS and installed by the aircrew.

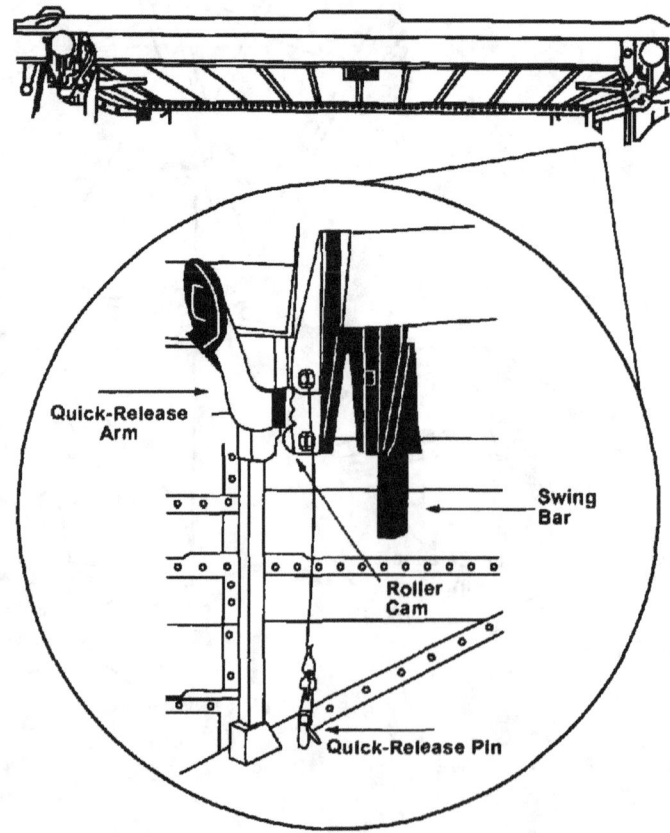

Figure 2-17. Fast Rope Anchor Bar.

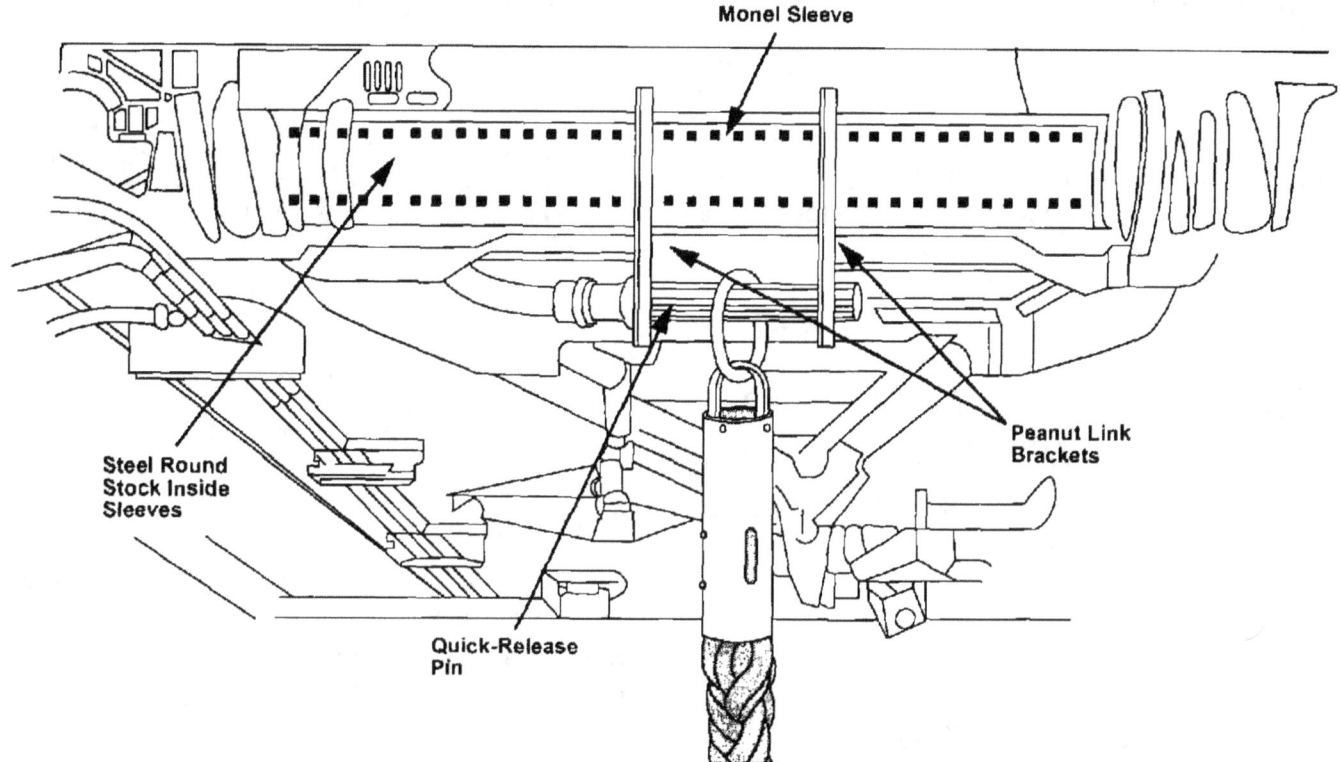

Figure 2-18. A-Frame Fast Rope Attachment Bar Assembly.

Knots

All knots used by ropers fall into four categories: end of the rope knots, anchor knots, middle of the rope knots, and specialty knots. The square knot, water tape knot, and the double fisherman's knot are end of rope knots. Anchor knots include the bowline, clove hitch, and round turn with two half hitches. The figure eight loop is a middle of the rope knot. Specialty knots include the overhand knot, end of the rope prussic, directional figure eight loop, military rappel seat, around the body bowline with figure eight, munter hitch, three loop bowline, and swami wrap.

End of Rope Knots

Square Knot

The square knot is used to join two ropes of equal diameter together. This knot is secured on each side by an overhand knot. Pigtails will be a minimum of 4 inches (see fig. 2-19).

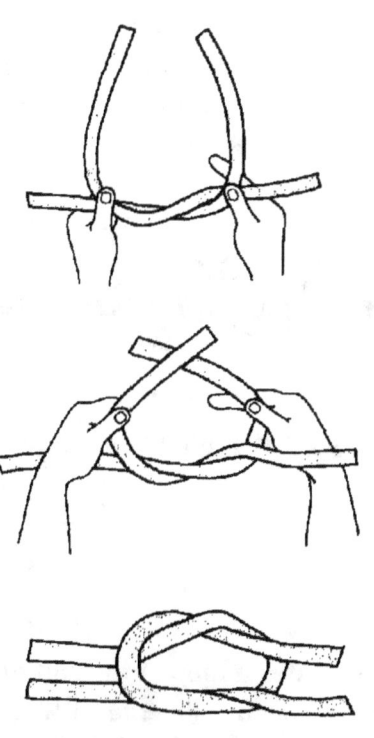

Figure 2-19. Square Knot.

Water Tape Knot

This knot is used to secure webbing or tape runners. It is constructed by tying an overhand knot (without twists) in one end of the tape and threading the other end of the tape through the knot from the opposite direction. Pigtails should be a minimum of 4 inches (see fig. 2-20).

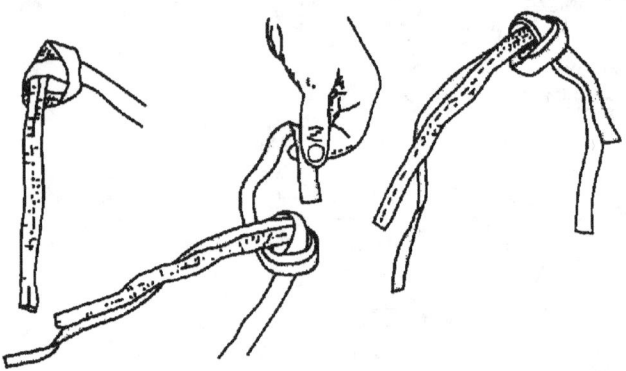

Figure 2-20. Water Tape Knot.

Double Fisherman's Knot

This knot joins two rope ends of equal thickness and is a strong joining knot. It is difficult to untie and is somewhat bulky. Pigtails should be a minimum of 4 inches (see fig. 2-21).

Figure 2-21. Double Fisherman's Knot.

Anchor Knots

Bowline

A bowline creates a loop at the end of a rope that can be used to secure the end of the rope around an object or anchor point. The pigtail must be inside and secured with an overhand knot. Pigtails will be a minimum of 4 inches. Rope loop

size will be approximately 1 to 12 inches in diameter (see fig. 2-22).

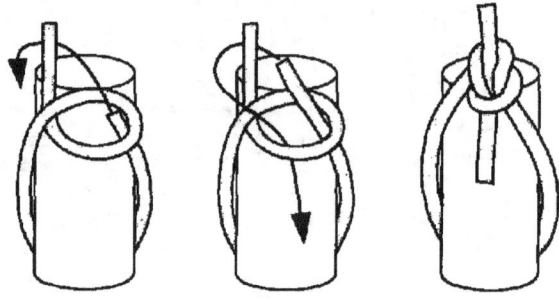

Figure 2-22. Bowline Knot.

Clove Hitch

The clove hitch is used to secure a rope to a round/cylindrical object (e.g., trees, poles, pipes). It is an equal tension knot. Pigtails will be a minimum of 4 inches (see fig. 2-23).

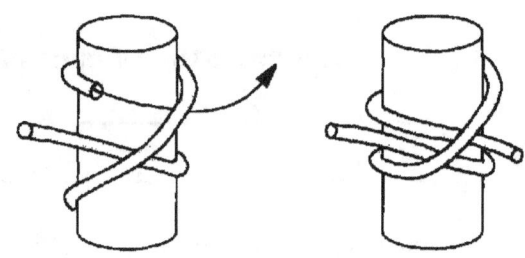

Figure 2-23. Clove Hitch.

Round Turn with Two Half Hitches

This knot forms a loop that runs around an object in such a manner as to provide 360 degree contact and may be used to distribute the load over a small diameter anchor. It is secured with two half hitches (see fig. 2-24).

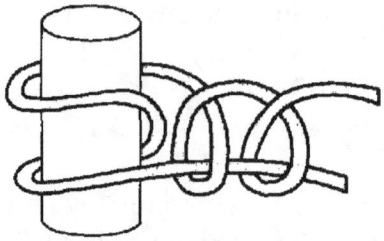

Figure 2-24. Round Turn with Two Half Hitches.

Middle of the Rope Knot: Figure Eight Loop

The figure eight loop forms a single bight and is used as an anchor in the middle or end of the rope. Pigtails will be a minimum of 4 inches. Rope loop size will be approximately 1 to 12 inches in diameter (see fig. 2-25).

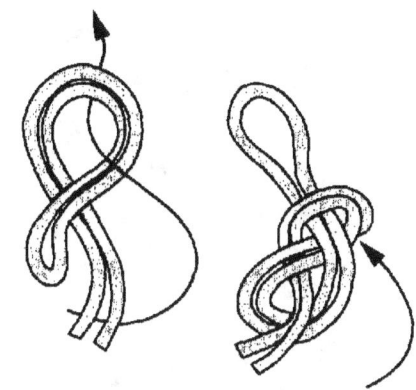

Figure 2-25. Figure Eight Loop.

Specialty Knots

Overhand Knot

The overhand knot is used to secure pigtails at the end of a primary knot (see fig. 2-26).

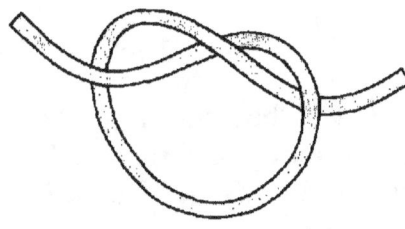

Figure 2-26. Overhand Knot.

End of the Rope Prussic

This knot moves freely along a fixed rope until tension is applied to it. Once tension is applied, the knot locks in place. It can be used as a safety/retrieval line. This knot is always secured with a bowline. Do not tie this knot with tape—it will

create less friction. Pigtails will be a minimum of 4 inches (see fig. 2-27).

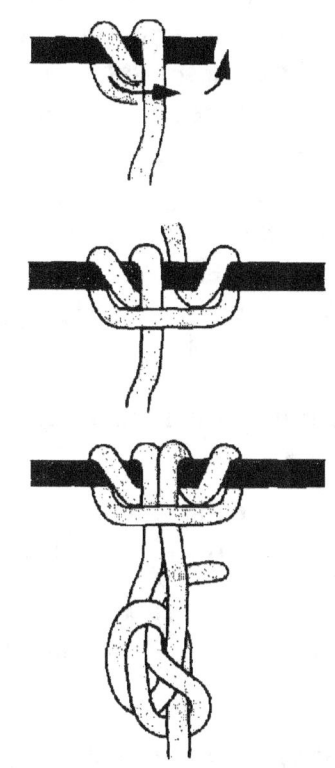

Figure 2-27. End of the Rope Prussic.

Directional Figure Eight Loop

The directional figure eight loop forms a single, fixed loop that can be tied so that the loop faces either the standing end or the running end. It may be used as a primary and secondary anchor. Rope loop size will be approximately 1 to 12 inches in diameter (see fig. 2-28).

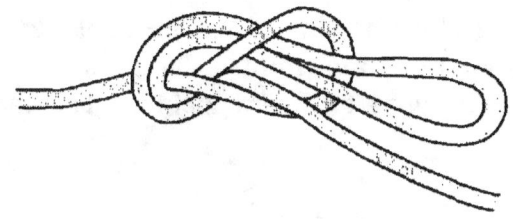

Figure 2-28. Directional Figure Eight Loop.

Military Rappel Seat

The military rappel seat is made from a sling rope:

- Take the center of the sling rope and place it on the left hip so that the running ends of the rope wrap around the waist just below the hip bone.
- Bring both ends together in front of the body.
- Tie an overhand knot with two wraps in front.
- Bring the two running ends down through the legs, up over the buttocks, and over the original waist wrap and the waist.
- Bring the rope over itself forming a bight, then cinch the rope up tightly.

    Note: The rope should run along the outside of the buttocks.

- Take the two running ends and make a square knot with two overhands on the left hip.

Any loose rope from the square knot is tucked into a pocket. Pigtails will be a minimum of 4 inches (see fig. 2-29).

Around the Body Bowline with Figure Eight

Around the body bowline is used as a secondary anchor point for SPIE rigging and also as a safety line for HRST operations. Pigtails will be a minimum of 4 inches (see fig. 2-30).

Munter Hitch

A munter hitch is a simple hitch in the rope that is clipped into the carabiner to put friction on the line (see fig. 2-31).

Three Loop Bowline

The three loop bowline is a single knot that forms three anchor loop points. The anchor knot is formed using part of the rappel line. This method

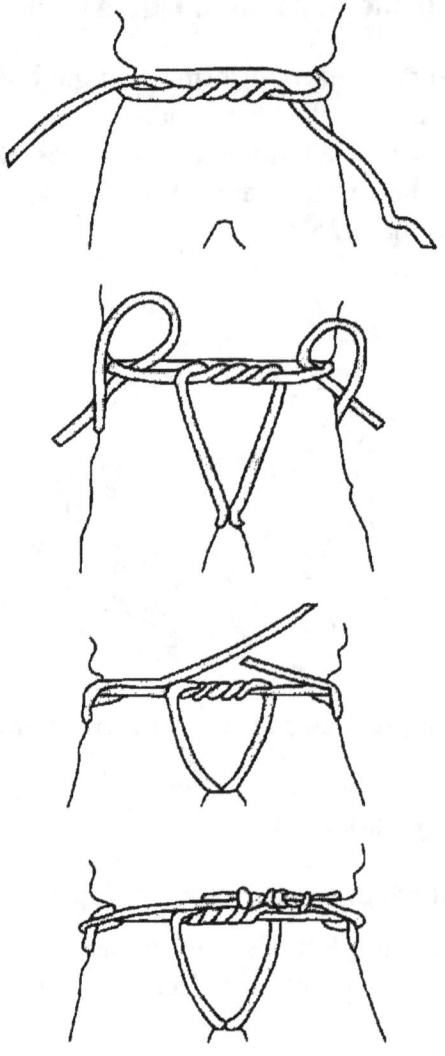

Figure 2-29. Military Rappel Seat.

is best used when the rappel rope is guided from the deck through overhead rigging. Rig the three loop bowline as follows (see fig. 2-32):

- Use one end of the rope and fold over approximately 10 feet of line. Adjust the length of the fold depending on the distance between the anchor points.

Figure 2-30. Around the Body Bowline with Figure Eight.

- Use the folded over portion and tie a bowline. Tie the bowline with the doubled line the same as a single line. The bowline will form two of the loops, while the running end will form the third loop.
- Attach all three loops to the attachment points using locking carabiners. Ensure the gates are facing up for easy inspection.
- Adjust all loops equally or as needed by taking in or letting out the third loop formed.
- Route the rappel line through a 10K carabiner that is attached to the overhead in order to provide for easier hook ups and exits.

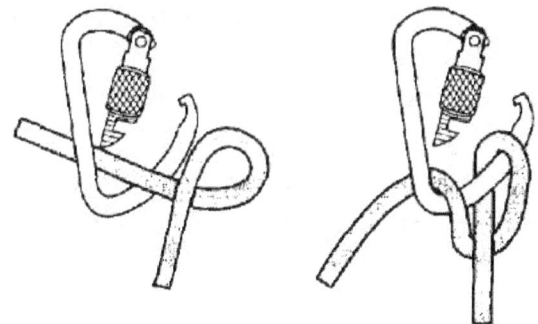

Figure 2-31. Munter Hitch.

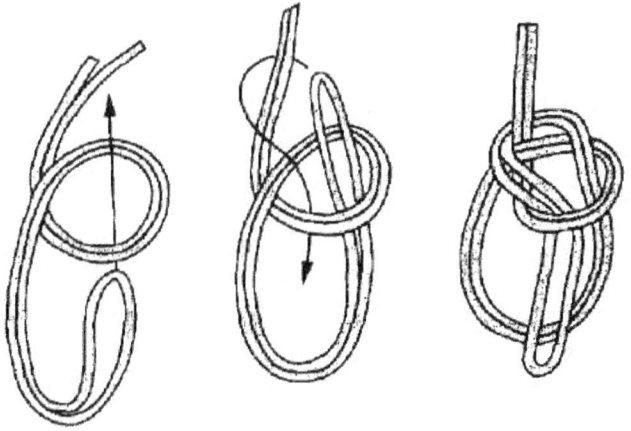

Figure 2-32. Three Loop Bowline.

Swami Wrap

The swami wrap is used as an anchor for fast rope systems. A swami wrap consists of a sling rope and a steel locking carbiner. Rig the swami wrap as follows:

- Place the middle of a sling rope over the anchor point.

- Create a minimum of seven full wraps around the anchor point.
- Place the carabiner in the center three wraps with the gate facing down, the gate locked.
- Fasten the free ends of the swami wrap with a square knot, tight across the top of the wrap.
- The square knot is secured with an overhand knot on both pigtails.
- Pigtails will be a minimum of 4 inches and a maximum length that is less than that required to complete one full wrap.

See figure 2-33.

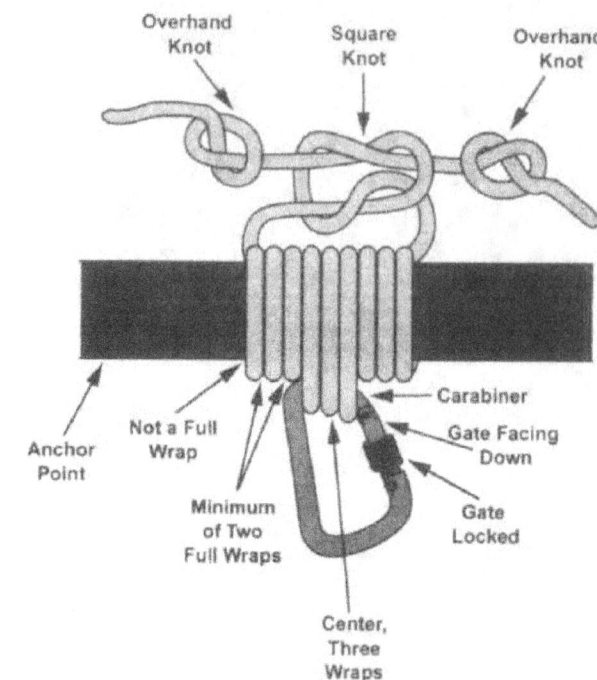

Figure 2-33. Swami Wrap.

CHAPTER 3
TOWER TRAINING

Tower training prepares Marines for HRST. This training provides the introduction to HRST and gradually introduces Marines to more demanding platforms. The static tower may vary in size and height from 30 to 90 feet. Marines who have met HRST static tower proficiency requirements and have the recommendation of the HRST master in charge of the static tower training phase may progress to the helicopter training phase. This chapter addresses tower training requirements and the transition to helicopter training.

Training Phases

The tower is used to introduce a Marine to HRST techniques and for refresher training. Each phase of rappel training, with and without gear, begins on a walled surface. HRST can also be taught by mounting a helicopter skid mock-up to the tower. The figure eight rappel may be taught on the tower when figure eight assault descenders are available.

Safety Personnel and Equipment

The following personnel and equipment are required during all static tower training:

- One SIO.
- One HRST master per rope station.
- One corpsman equipped with medical bag, cervical collar, and backboard with straps.

Note: The corpsman will not participate as a roper.

- One safety vehicle with driver. The driver will not participate as a roper.
- One belay man per rope station. Ropers will alternate stations.

Preparation

Rappel

All rappel rope stations are rigged with three anchor points using the appropriate knots. All anchor points must be certified as being load tested to 5,000 pounds. Any slack is removed between the knots to create equal tension on all three anchor points. Ten feet of rope will be on the deck during tower rappelling for belay purposes.

Fast Rope

All fast rope stations are rigged with two anchor points. All anchor points must be certified as being load tested to 5,000 pounds per roper on the rope at one time (e.g., single roper equals 5,000 pound test, two ropers equal 10,000 pound test). Ten feet of rope will be on the deck at all times during tower fast roping to assist in anchoring the running end of the rope.

Inspection

The HRST master is in charge of the tower, and he is responsible for visually and physically inspecting the tower. Appendix E provides tower inspection standards.

Safety Procedures

The following safety procedures apply to all training on the tower:

- The tower will not be utilized during thunderstorms or excessively high winds. If ice is present or if the platform is slick from rain, HRST training will be delayed until conditions are safe.
- A roper will not carry anything in his hands while climbing the ladder.
- There will only be one roper on each ladder at any given time.
- The HRST master or SIO determines how many ropers per rope station is safe.
- The HRST master and SIO must be aware of ropers who appear to be experiencing uneasiness with heights and train ropers only to their confidence level.
- The HRST master or SIO will re-inspect each roper's equipment for proper donning and serviceability prior to the roper ascending the tower and prior to descending the rope.
- The HRST master is secured to the tower with a safety line. The length of the safety line will not exceed the amount necessary to perform his duties.
- A roper will not descend the rope without proper gloves and a helmet.
- At no time shall any participant step on a rope.
- Bounding is not permitted due to the stress it places on the ropes and anchor points.

Conduct of Training

Safety Brief

Prior to commencement of any training, the HRST master conducts a tower safety brief. The safety brief includes tower commands and proper roping techniques (see app. F).

Demonstration

After explaining tower procedures to all ropers, an assistant demonstrates one complete cycle of training on the tower. This allows the ropers to hear the HRST master issue the proper commands and see the actions and proper techniques used on the static tower.

Tower Rappel Procedures

Once directed to a rope station, the HRST master ensures proper hook up for rappelling.

While maintaining his brake, the roper, on command from the HRST master, steps to the edge and faces the anchor point.

The roper sounds off his name "Jones on rappel." The belay man responds with his name "Smith on belay."

On direction from the HRST master, the roper assumes the L-shaped position (see fig. 3-1).

Figure 3-1. L-Shaped Position.

On the command "*Go*" from the HRST master, the roper begins his descent.

The belay man places the rappel rope high in his upper back, under his armpits. He holds the standing end with his weak hand and the running end with his strong hand. If the roper loses control, the belay man positions the running end of the rope on his chest and runs backwards to stop the roper from falling. The belay man will not wear gloves and must keep his eyes on the roper at all times.

Once the roper is on the ground, the belay man grabs the rope in front of the roper and holds it as the roper walks backwards.

The roper's hands are placed above the carabiner to prevent being hit in the face with the end of the rope.

Once clear of the rope, the roper sounds off his name "Jones off rappel," and does a side-straddle hop.

Once the roper has cleared the rope, the belay man sounds off his name "Smith off belay."

Tower Skid Rappel

The tower skid rappel prepares Marines to rappel from a UH-1N helicopter. Proper training and safety procedures are the responsibility of the HRST master.

The roper is hooked up while he sits on the platform just above the helicopter skid.

After sounding off, and on command from the HRST master, the roper steps out onto the skid, turns around, and assumes an L-shaped position (see fig. 3-1).

On command, the roper pushes out and descends.

Tower Fast Rope Procedures

Ropers execute a descent at speeds commensurate with their experience/proficiency in fast rope operations.

Once directed to a rope station by the HRST master, the roper assumes a seated or standing position. The HRST master ensures that positive control of the roper is maintained until the individual roper has engaged the fast rope.

The HRST master ensures that the proper safety equipment is donned by each roper.

The HRST master directs the roper to engage the fast rope with the voice command "*Feet, hands*" for a seated fast rope descent or "*Hands*" for a standing fast rope execution.

On command from the HRST master, the roper approaches the fast rope and grasps it with both hands and feet. **Never jump for a rope.**

The HRST master taps the first roper on the back of the head while giving the voice command "*Go.*"

The individual roper executes a 45 to 90 degree turn and descends the rope.

While executing a fast rope, the roper keeps his hands at face level. The rate of descent is adjusted by hand, knee, and foot pressure on the rope.

Note: The roper does not descend hand-over-hand. The rope slides through gloved hands.

During descent, the roper looks down at the ground and the ropers below.

The roper will not wrap feet and legs around the rope. Feet and legs hang with the rope passing between the arches of the feet (see fig. 3-2).

Figure 3-2. Fast Rope Technique.

If the hands start to burn, the roper will not let go of the rope; instead he applies more feet and knee pressure.

The roper executes a fast rope landing. At approximately 3 to 5 feet from the ground, the roper spreads his legs roughly shoulder-width apart, keeping his knees slightly bent to absorb the landing. If the landing is poorly executed and the roper falls to the ground, he immediately releases the rope and rolls out of the landing area.

The HRST master ensures the tensile strength of the anchor point is not exceeded.

During descent, a roper may lock in to preclude landing on a fallen roper by standing on the fast rope. To lock in, slide one foot on the top of the other with the rope placed between the feet. A wringing action with the hands on the rope assists in a positive lock in.

CHAPTER 4
HELICOPTER RAPPELLING OPERATIONS

Rappelling is the technique used to lower oneself down a rope quickly when fast rope equipment is not available or when the load carried by the roper is too heavy to permit safe fast rope operations. Marines rappel from a hovering helicopter as a means of insertion when terrain, vegetation, or the tactical situation do not allow for landing. This chapter establishes the basic guidelines for conducting helicopter rappelling operations and training Marines in helicopter rappelling techniques.

Familiarization

A thorough briefing is required for all users before rappelling operations are conducted. The brief should consist of, but not be restricted to, a review of all the equipment associated with rappelling, loading of personnel, helicopter approach, deplaning, descent, commands and signals, and preflight and in-flight safety procedures. For deplaning, it is essential that personnel receive the necessary training in rappelling techniques before using rappelling on a tactical mission. When time and the situation permit, unqualified personnel are allowed to watch a rappelling operation or to participate in the installation of equipment on the helicopter in order to get familiar with both the equipment and rappelling techniques. Ropers unfamiliar with rappelling initially conduct training without combat equipment until confidence and skill level warrant more difficult operations.

Safety

All rappelling operations are preceded by a safety brief. The safety brief should consist of, but not be limited to, a review of all the equipment associated with rappelling, insertion methods, and, most importantly, emergency procedures (see apps. A and B). The following safety measures are taken during rappelling operations.

Required Personnel and Equipment

The following is a list of personnel and equipment that is required prior to conducting rappelling training:

- One SIO.
- One HRST master per aircraft in the UH-1N and H-60 or one HRST master per rope station in the CH-46E, CH-53D/E, and H-47.
- One corpsman equipped with medical bag, cervical collar, and backboard with straps. The corpsman will not participate as a roper.
- One safety vehicle with driver. The driver will not participate as a roper.
- Radio communications with personnel in the insert zone.
- One belay man. The belay man holds the rope to steady it for the ropers. When belaying out of a helicopter, the belay man positions himself under the exit point so as not to inadvertently slow or stop the roper prematurely (see fig. 4-1 on page 4-2).

Rope Deployment Methods

There are two types of rope deployment methods: circular loop and rope deployment bag. To create a circular loop, coil the rope in a round coil as it is being placed in a waterproof bag. Make sure to coil from running end first, finishing at the standing end. DO NOT tie any knots at the end of the rope or secure the rope to the bag in any fashion. The rope deployment bag deploys the rope in an orderly manner. The rope is back-stacked into the bag in an S-type manner, starting with the running end and working to the standing end. DO NOT tie or secure the rope to the deployment bag in any way.

Figure 4-1. Belay Man.

—————————— WARNING ——————————

Attaching any object or weight to the running end of any rope is prohibited. Objects attached to a rope could prevent a roper from freeing himself from the rope in the event of an emergency.

To counter the effects of rotor downwash, a minimum of 15 to 20 feet of rope on the ground can act as a rope weight.

Rigging/Hook Up

All helicopters rig for rappelling in the same basic manner. No helicopter modifications are necessary for rappel rigging. Two basic requirements are mandatory when rigging for rappelling: redundancy of attachment points and adequate padding to ensure no damage to the ropes. The HRST master is responsible for properly rigging the helicopter and he personally inspects all rappel rigging. Rappelling can be conducted from the UH-1N, CH-46E, CH-53D/E, H-47, and H-60 helicopters. Rigging the H-47 and H-60 helicopters may use equipment that is not organic to the Marine Corps. The gear in these procedures is organic to the aircraft assets that may be provided by the other Services.

Rigging the UH-1N

The UH-1N's rope stations are located on the port and starboard side. The UH-1N's rappel system uses three cargo tie down fittings, located on the floor, as anchor points for each rope station. Each UH-1N's rope station has two rappelling ropes and three steel locking carabiners in a three-point, one-directional fixed assembly. The assembly allows quick installation and removal while maintaining safety. Only one tie down fitting is used per deck plate; the fittings must be in a straight line. To rig the UH-1N—

- Attach three steel locking carabiners to the three separate cargo tie down fittings.
- With the running end of the two rappel lines departing the helicopter, attach each rappel line to the primary anchor point with a directional figure eight.
- Attach each rappel line to the secondary anchor point with a directional figure eight.
- Attach each rappel line to the tertiary anchor point with a figure eight loop.
- Ensure there is equal tension between the primary and secondary anchor points and the secondary and tertiary anchor points.
- Lock all carabiners.
- Pad the edge of the cabin deck to cover sharp edges or metal burrs in order to prevent rappel line chaffing.

—————————— WARNING ——————————

Only one roper shall be on a rappel rope at one time. The load limitation of the cargo tie down rings precludes total weight in excess of 500 pounds to be applied to any single tie down ring. It is ideal to send a roper from both the left and right skid at the same time. This helps maintain stability of the helicopter during HRST operations.

Rigging the CH-46E

There are four stations on the CH-46E that can be rigged for rappelling. The helicopter ramp can be rigged both port and starboard, the hell hole, and the crew door. All stations use three anchor points to secure the rope.

Ramp Rope Station

The ramp rope station is rigged by using two directional figure eight loops and a figure eight loop. The primary and secondary anchor points are each secured with a directional figure eight loop and the tertiary anchor point is tied with a double figure eight loop. All anchor knots are secured to cargo tie down rings by a locking carabiner. The ramp is padded to protect the ropes from becoming cut. The edges of the side of the ramp are also padded and taped. Personnel rappelling from the ramp rope station must ensure that they exit straight back from the ramp and not at an angle in order to prevent the rope from getting caught on the side of the ramp.

Hell Hole Station

To rig the hell hole rope station, the internal winch overhead pulley attachment point is used as the primary anchor. A carabiner is attached to this point after measuring the briefed hover altitude plus 20 feet from the running end, then a directional figure eight is tied and the loop is attached to the carabiner, redirect the standing rope through the carabiner to the second anchor point (see fig. 4-2). The second anchor may be one of four deck rings located next to the hell hole, two on each side. If rigging aft, the second anchor is the aft deck ring next to the hell hole. A carabiner is attached to the deck ring. The second anchor knot is a directional figure eight with the redirect through the carabiner. The tertiary anchor is the second deck ring in the direction you are rigging. The tertiary anchor knot is a figure eight loop.

Note: This system can be rigged port or starboard forward or aft of the hell hole.

Crew Door Station

To rappel from the crew door, the door may remain in the down position or be placed in the locked position under the helicopter. The primary anchor is the starboard deck ring directly inside the crew door. The primary anchor knot is a directional figure eight. The second anchor is the outboard port side deck ring directly across and slightly aft of the primary anchor. The secondary anchor knot is a directional figure eight with the redirect running through the carabiner. The tertiary anchor point is the second deck ring aft of the secondary anchor. The tertiary anchor

Figure 4-2. CH-46E Hell Hole Station Anchor Points.

knot is a figure eight loop. All anchor knots are attached to the cargo tie down rings by a closed and locked carabiner. All edges of the crew door in contact with the rope are padded and taped.

Rigging the CH-53D/E

The CH-53 helicopter is the least desired platform to rappel from due to rotor wash, but it can be used for HRST. The ramp and hell hole are rigged the same as the CH-46E. In order to get into the L-shaped position, personnel rappelling from the ramp rope station must ensure that they exit straight back from the ramp and not at an angle in order to prevent the rope from getting caught on the side of the ramp.

Rigging the H-47 Helicopter

There are two variants of the H-47 helicopter that may be used by the Marine Corps. The US Army flies both variants (the CH-47 and the MH-47).

Rope Stations

There are two rappelling stations in the H-47 that can be used to support rappelling operations. They are the crew door and the ramp; both utilize a fast rope bar as the primary anchor point.

Ramp and Crew Door Station

Both the ramp and the crew door stations utilize the fast rope bar for the primary anchor point. The aircraft squadron is responsible for the installation and setup of the fast rope bar. The secondary and tertiary anchor points are the next available cargo tie downs. If rigging the self-equalizing setup or pre-equalized cordelette with the rescue rope, the three anchor points are the tie downs closest to the exit point. The rappel rope then routes through a 10K carabiner attached to the fast rope bar. All anchor points should have equal tension and be on different deck plates

when possible. Rigging the ramp or crew door for rappelling is as follows:

- Attach a 10K locking carabiner to the fast rope bar and lock it.
- If using an optional rescue rope setup, install the self-equalizing setup (see page 4-5) or the pre-equalized cordelette (see page 4-6). Join the ends of the rescue rope and rappel rope together and attach the rescue rope to the attachment point. See page 4-7 for the rescue rope setup. Run the rescue rope through the carabiner attached to the fast rope bar.
- If no rescue rope setup is used, attach the rope to the 10K carabiner on the fast rope bar using a figure eight on a bight. Ensure there is enough rope standing end to attach to the next two points. Tie a directional figure eight for the second anchor point. Tie either a bowline or figure eight for the third anchor point.
- Ensure all gates on the locking carabiners are locked and facing up for easy inspection.
- Ensure the crew door is secured back if rappelling from this station.
- Pad and tape all edges that come in contact with the rope.

Rigging the H-60 Helicopter

There are four variants of the H-60 helicopter that can be used by Marine Corps personnel:

- HH-60 and SH-60 are flown by the US Navy.
- UH-60 is flown by the US Army.
- MH-60 is flown by Air Force Special Operations Command (AFSOC).
- HH-60J is flown by the Coast Guard.

The HH-60 and SH-60 are single door aircraft, and the UH-60 and MH-60 are double door aircraft.

Rope Stations

The rope station supporting H-60 rappel operations is the side door. Each side door can be rigged for two rappel stations (one forward and one aft). The UH-60 and MH-60 can be configured for both doors. The HH-60 and SH-60 are both single door aircraft and are configured on the starboard side only. All anchor points should have equal tension when the load is placed on the rope.

Side Door Station (Single Door)

Because ropers will only be exiting on the starboard side of the aircraft, the ropes can be rigged using the port side deck cargo tie down rings. The three anchor points are two center deck rings and one port side deck ring. Rigging the single door H-60 is as follows (see fig. 4-3).

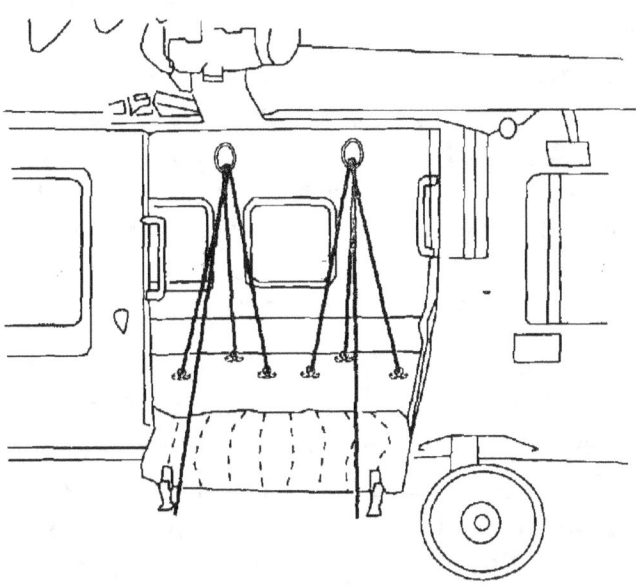

Figure 4-3. SH-60 Rigged for Rappel (no rescue rope installed).

• If using optional rescue rope setup, install the self-equalizing setup (see the paragraph in the next column) or the pre-equalized cordelette (see page 4-6). Run the rescue rope through the forward port then starboard upper cargo rings and join the ends of the rescue rope and rappel rope together. Attach the rescue rope to the attachment point. Ensure the joining knot is located on the running side (rappel side) of the

upper tie down rings. See page 4-7 for the rescue rope setup.

• If a rescue rope setup is not used, route the rappel rope through the forward starboard then port upper cargo rings. Attach the rope to the anchor points utilizing the three-loop bowline method, self-equalizing setup (see the paragraph in the next column), or the pre-equalized cordelette (see page 4-6).

• A second rappel station can be rigged using the aft port and starboard upper cargo rings and separate deck rings.

• Ensure all gates on the locking carabiners are locked and facing up for easy inspection.

• Pad and tape all edges coming in contact with the rope and ensure side door is locked open.

Side Door Station (Double Door)

When configuring a double door H-60 for both doors, three anchor points are required for each rope station. Because of limited cabin space, only the overhead cargo rings are utilized for double door rigging. Rigging for each station of the double door H-60 is follows:

• Tie a directional figure eight 4 feet from the end of the standing end of the rope and attach to the overhead cargo ring (closest to the exit) using a locking carabiner.

• Tie a bowline or figure eight 2 feet from the primary anchor point and attach to the secondary overhead cargo ring (inboard of exit) using a locking carabiner.

• Pad and tape all edges coming in contact with the rope and ensure side door is locked open.

Self-Equalizing Setup

This method provides three self-equalized attachment points and uses none of the rappel rope to construct the rigging. It can be used with or without the rescue rope setup. The anchor points can be in any configuration or distance apart. The self-equalizing setup is best used when the rappel rope is guided from the deck through overhead rigging. Rigging the self-equalized setup is as follows (see fig. 4-4):

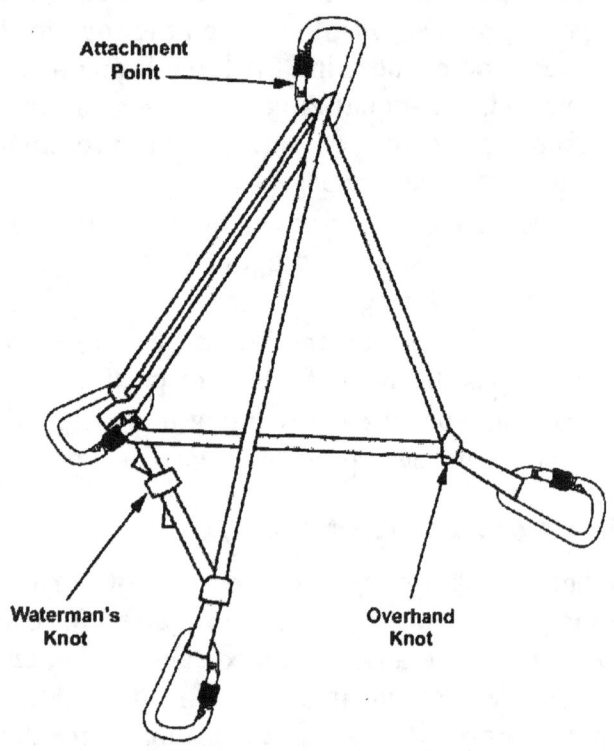

Figure 4-4. Self-Equalizing Setup.

- Cut a piece of 1 inch tubular nylon or rappel rope to an approximate length of 20 feet, depending on the anchor point separations.
- Tie the ends of the 1 inch nylon together using a watertape knot, leaving 3 inches to 6 inches of pigtail. If using rappel rope, tie the ends using a rethreaded figure eight.
- Hold loop flat to make an oval with the knot toward one end.
- Tie an overhand knot 3 inches from end of the oval to form a second loop.
- Keep knots even and repeat the overhand knot on the opposite side.
- Attach the loop closest to the watertape knot to the first attachment point using locking carabiner with the gate facing up.
- Twist the oval a half a turn to form an "X" in the middle.

- Attach other end loop to second attachment point using carabiner.
- Attach center of "X" to third attachment point using locking carabiner.
- Attach a fourth locking carabiner to center of "X." This is the rappel line attachment point.
- Attach the rappel line to the carabiner using a bowline knot or rescue rope setup.
- Route the rappel line through a 10K carabiner attached to the overhead. This routes the rappel line off the deck to provide for easier hook ups and exits.

Pre-Equalized Cordelette

This method provides three pre-equalized attachment points and uses none of the rappel rope to construct the rigging. It can be used with or without the rescue rope setup. The anchor points can be in any configuration or distance apart. The pre-equalizing cordelette can be used with the rappel rope guided from the deck through the overhead rigging. Rigging the pre-equalized cordelette is as follows (see fig. 4-5):

- Cut a piece of 1 inch tubular nylon or rappel rope to an approximate length of 20 feet, depending on the an-chor point separations.
- Tie the ends of the 1 inch nylon together using a watertape knot to form a continuous loop. Leave 3 to 6 inches of pigtail. If using rappel rope, tie ends using a rethreaded figure eight, leaving a minimum of 4 inches of pigtail.
- Attach the loop to each of the three anchor points using a locking carabiner for each with the gate facing up and locked. Position the knot that secures the loop close to an anchor point.
- Pull the three rope sections between the anchor points and gather them together to form three bights. Ensure the bights all have equal tension when pulled in the direction of the rappel. Ensure the knot that secures the loop is still positioned close to an anchor point and not in the bights.

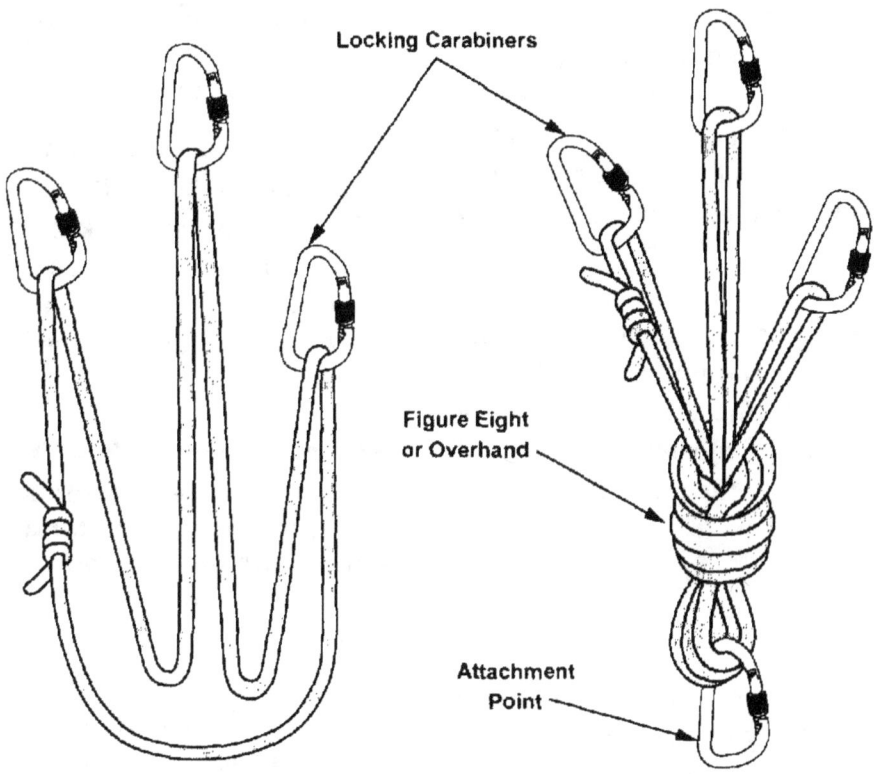

Figure 4-5. Pre-eqalized Cordelette.

- Make a figure eight knot or overhand knot with the three bights and attach a 10K locking carabiner to this point. This is the attachment point for the rappel line.
- Attach the rappel line to the carabiner using a bowline or rescue rope setup.
- Route the rappel line through a 10K carabiner attached to the overhead. This routes the rappel line off the deck to provide for easier hook ups and exits.

Rescue Rope Setup

The rescue rope setup is an optional method used to lower the rappeller if he becomes entangled. It is used with the self-equalizing setup and the pre-equalized cordelette.

The rescue rope must be the same or within 2mm difference of the rappel line used. This helps ensure a stronger, more uniform knot at the junction with the rappel line. Rigging procedures for attachment of the rescue rope to the equalizing attachment point are as follows (see fig. 4-6 on p. 4-8):

- Join the ends of the rescue rope and rappel rope using a rethreaded figure eight. Use an overhand knot to join the ropes if the knot is positioned before any guiding carabiners (i.e., hoist). The overhand knot can slip through a carabiner if needed.
- Clip the rescue rope through the 10K attachment carabiner of the self-equalizing or pre-equalized anchor. Ensure the joining knot between the rescue and rappel ropes is on the rappelling side of the carabiner.
- Tie a releasable knot system on the 10K attachment carabiner using the rescue rope. The releasable knot is tied with a munter hitch, a mule knot, and an overhand knot. Load the munter hitch to the correct position before the mule and overhand knots are tied. The mule and overhand knots are tied to the running end (rappel side) of the rope.

- Ensure the carabiner with the releasable knot is in line with the rappel and not at an angle.
- Tie a figure eight on a bight to the standing end of the rescue rope and attach to a hard point in the aircraft. This prevents the rescue rope from being fed through completely when lowering the rappeller.
- Gain control of the standing end of the rescue rope, remove the overhand knot and pull on the rescue rope to release the mule knot. Slowly lower the rappeller to the ground. The crew chief or assistant HRST master must call out the remaining distance to the ground.

Hook Up

To hook up—

- The HRST master reaches down and grabs the running end of the rope with his left hand.
- The HRST master calls the roper forward.
- The roper faces the HRST master and places his left hand on the HRST master's right shoulder.
- The HRST master instructs the roper to grab the running end of the rope (right hand, palm down, thumb toward body) just below the HRST master's left hand. This acts as the roper's brake hand.

Note: A left-hand wrap for the left-handed rappel is not authorized. All ropers will brake with the right hand.

- The roper places the running end of the rope in the small of his back.
- The HRST master takes the standing end of the rope and snaps it down into the carabiner, wraps that end around the bottom (solid end) of the carabiner, and snaps it down into the carabiner again.

─────────── **WARNING** ───────────

Should the rope be wrapped from the running end rather than the standing end, the rappel system will fail and serious injury may occur.

─────────────────────────────

- The carabiner gate is then locked shut.
- The HRST master instructs the roper to lean back and test the brake.
- Upon command from the HRST master, the roper assumes the L-shaped position (feet shoulder width apart, knees locked, upper body bent slightly forward).
- The HRST master gives the command "*Go.*"
- The roper looks over his right shoulder, throws his right arm out to the side, and loosens his

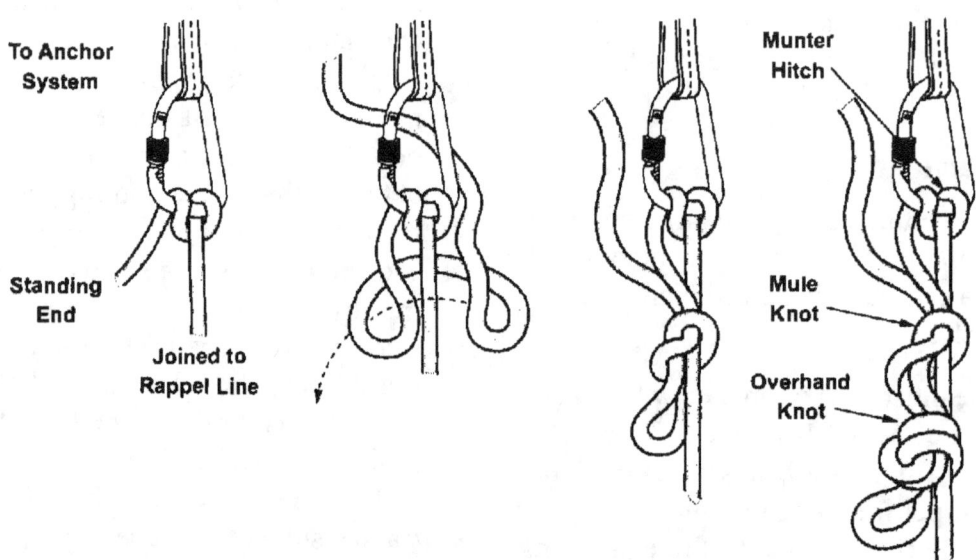

Figure 4-6. Rescue Rope Tied to Anchor System.

grip, which allows the rope to slide through his hand and allows him to descend.

- The roper proceeds to rappel using his left hand as a guide hand on the rope between himself and the anchor point and his right hand as the brake.

- The roper must ensure that all loose clothing near the carabiner is tucked in tightly to prevent it from becoming entangled in the carabiner.

Roper Responsibilities

Roper responsibilities are as follows:

- Understand and comply with all aspects of HRST and emergency procedures.
- Ensure all safety equipment is properly donned and inspected by an HRST master.
- Ensure seat belts are hooked-up prior to takeoff and unbuckle only on command of the HRST master.
- Maintain eye contact with the HRST master at all times prior to beginning a descent.
- Make deliberate movements toward the rope station while maintaining a hand hold in the helicopter at all times. ·
- Grasp ropes firmly when directed by the HRST master.
- Control descent speeds and brake to avoid injury.
- Look down at the ground while descending.
- Move rapidly away from the rope upon landing.

Sequence of Events

Note: HRST master's ICS calls are bold italic.

CH-46E and CH-53E Hell Hole Rappel

A hell hole rappel from either the CH-46E or the CH-53E is executed as follows:

Load on command from the crew chief and inspect the installation of the rappel rope.

The HRST master dons a gunner's belt and performs an ICS check.

"ICS check."

Once the aircraft commander responds, the HRST master acknowledges, *"I have you loud and clear"* or *"I have you the same"* or *"I have you weak."*

Once all ropers are seated and strapped in, the HRST master notifies the crew chief that *"Ropers are ready."*

The crew chief clears the aircraft commander for departure.

After takeoff, the ropers remain strapped in and the HRST master remains oriented through periodic updates from the aircraft commander.

Once the aircraft commander gives the *"2-minute"* warning, the HRST master responds, *"Roger, 2 minutes."*

The HRST master holds up two fingers and each roper holds up two fingers on each gloved hand to indicate the *"2-minute"* command.

The HRST master ensures that each roper has his helmet, eye protection, and gloves and is ready to go.

The crew chief assists the HRST master by opening the hell hole door.

> *Note:* At no time will the HRST master leave an open rope station unattended.

The aircraft commander gives the *"1-minute"* call.

The HRST master responds, *"Roger, 1 minute."*

The HRST master gives the *"1-minute"* command to the ropers using hand-and-arm signals.

Ropers make final checks of all gear.

Once the helicopter is in a stable hover, the aircraft commander gives the command *"Deploy the rope."*

When the HRST master can see the target directly below, he responds, *"Roger, deploy the rope."*

The HRST master verifies that the rope is not fouled, on the deck, and on target, then he tells the aircraft commander *"Rope on the deck."*

The HRST master uses hand-and-arm signals to command a roper to *"Unbuckle"* and *"Take position."*

These commands are directed to one roper. All others remain seated and strapped in until told to unbuckle and take position.

The HRST master ensures that he has physical control of the roper to prevent loss of balance and falling out of the helicopter. The HRST master maintains this control until the roper is sent out and begins his descent down the rope.

Once the HRST master has connected a roper to the rope, he tells the aircraft commander *"First man on rope."*

The HRST master verifies that the belay man is set (unless self-belay system is being used).

The HRST master directs the roper to the exit point and has him assume the hanging or sitting position over the hell hole.

The HRST master gives the roper the *"Go"* hand-and-arm signal.

The HRST master assists the roper in clearing his gear as the roper lowers himself through the hell hole.

The HRST master monitors the roper all the way to the deck.

Continue on with remaining ropers.

The HRST master ensures that after each roper is on the deck the belay man is reset before sending out the next roper.

When the last roper is off the rope, the HRST master tells the aircraft commander *"Last man off rope"* and *"Rope being pulled to the 6 o'clock* (whichever was briefed) *position"* or *"Rope retrieved."*

CH-46E, CH-53D/E, and H-47 Ramp Rappel

To execute a ramp rappel from either a CH-46E, CH-53D/E, or H-47—

Load on command from the crew chief and inspect the installation of the rappel rope.

Don your gunner's belt and perform an ICS check.

"ICS check."

Once the aircraft commander responds, the HRST master acknowledges, *"I have you loud and clear"* or *"I have you the same"* or *"I have you weak."*

Once all ropers are seated and strapped in, the HRST master notifies the crew chief that *"Ropers are ready."*

The crew chief clears the aircraft commander for departure.

After take off, the ropers remain strapped in and the HRST master remains oriented through periodic updates from the aircraft commander.

Once the aircraft commander gives the *"2-minute"* warning, the HRST master responds, *"Roger, 2 minutes."*

The HRST master holds up two fingers and each roper holds up two fingers on each gloved hand to indicate the *"2-minute"* command.

The HRST master ensures that each roper has his helmet, eye protection, and gloves and is ready to go.

For ramp operations, the crew chief assists the HRST master by opening the ramp to the desired position.

Note: At no time will the HRST master leave an open rope station unattended.

The aircraft commander gives the *"1-minute"* call.

The HRST master responds, *"Roger, 1 minute."*

The HRST master gives the *"1-minute"* command to the ropers using hand-and-arm signals.

Ropers make final checks of all gear.

Once the helicopter is in a stable hover, the aircraft commander gives the command *"Deploy the rope."*

When the HRST master can see the target directly below, he responds, *"Roger, deploy the rope."*

Once the helicopter is in a stable hover, and the HRST master can see the target directly below, he deploys the rope.

The HRST master verifies that the rope is not fouled, on the deck, and on target, then he tells the aircraft commander *"Rope on the deck."*

The HRST master uses hand-and-arm signals to command a roper to *"Unbuckle"* and *"Take position"* at the edge of the ramp. These commands are directed to one roper. All others remain seated and strapped in until told to unbuckle and take position.

The HRST master ensures that he has physical control of the roper to prevent him from losing his balance and falling out of the helicopter. The HRST master maintains this control until the roper is sent out and begins his descent down the rope.

The HRST master hooks the roper into the system, tells the aircraft commander "*First man on rope*," physically controls the roper to the edge of the ramp, and verifies the belay man is set (unless a self-belay system is being used).

The HRST master uses hand-and-arm signals to direct the roper to assume the L-shaped position over the edge and continues giving the roper the L position sign until he is ready to send him.

The HRST master gives the roper the "*Go*" hand-and-arm signal.

The roper pushes out and descends from the helicopter and starts his rappel.

The HRST master monitors the roper all the way to the deck.

Continue on with remaining ropers.

The HRST master ensures that after each roper is on the deck the belay man is reset before sending out the next roper.

When the last roper is off the rope, the HRST master tells the aircraft commander "*Last man off rope*," and "*Rope being pulled to the 6 o'clock* (or whichever was briefed) *position*" or "*Rope retrieved*."

CH-46E, CH-53D, and H-47 Crew Door Rappel

To execute a crew door rappel from a CH-46E, CH-53D, or H-47—

Load on command from the crew chief and inspect the installation of the rappel rope.

Don your gunner's belt and perform an ICS check.

"*ICS check*."

Once the aircraft commander responds, the HRST master acknowledges, "*I have you loud and clear*" or "*I have you the same*" or "*I have you weak*."

Once all ropers are seated and strapped in, the HRST master notifies the crew chief that "*Ropers are ready*."

The crew chief clears the aircraft commander for departure.

After take off, the ropers remain strapped in and the HRST master remains oriented through periodic updates from the aircraft commander.

Once the aircraft commander gives the "*2-minute*" warning, the HRST master responds, "*Roger, 2 minutes*."

The HRST master holds up two fingers and each roper holds up two fingers on each gloved hand to indicate the "*2-minute*" command.

The HRST master ensures that each roper has his helmet, eye protection, and gloves and is ready to go.

For crew door operations, the crew chief assists the HRST master by opening the crew door.

> *Note:* At no time will the HRST master leave an open rope station unattended.

The aircraft commander gives the "*1-minute*" call.

The HRST master responds, "*Roger, 1 minute*."

The HRST master gives the "*1-minute*" command to the ropers using hand-and-arm signals.

Ropers make final checks of all gear.

Once the helicopter is in a stable hover the aircraft commander gives the command "*Deploy the rope*."

When the HRST master can see the target directly below, he responds, "*Roger, deploy the rope*."

Once the helicopter is in a stable hover and the HRST master can see the target directly below, he deploys the rope.

The HRST master verifies that the rope is not fouled, on the deck, and on target, then he tells the aircraft commander "*Rope on the deck*."

The HRST master uses hand-and-arm signals to command a roper to "*Unbuckle*" and "*Take position*" at the edge of the crew door exit. These commands are directed to one roper. All others remain seated and strapped in until told to unbuckle and take position.

The HRST master blocks the opening of the crew door prior to hooking up the roper.

The HRST master ensures that he has physical control of the roper to prevent loss of balance and falling out of the helicopter. The HRST master maintains this control until the roper is sent out and begins his descent down the rope.

The HRST master hooks the roper into the system, tells the aircraft commander, "*First man on the rope*," physically controls the roper to the edge of the bottom step of the crew door or the edge of the helicopter (if the crew door is removed), and verifies the belay man is set (unless a self-belay system is being used).

The HRST master uses hand-and-arm signals to direct the roper to assume the L-shaped position over the edge and continues giving the roper the L position signal until he is ready to send him.

The HRST master gives the roper the "*Go*" hand-and-arm signal.

The roper pushes out and descends from the helicopter and starts his rappel.

The HRST master monitors the roper all the way to the deck.

Continue on with remaining ropers.

The HRST master ensures that after each roper is on the deck the belay man is reset before sending out the next roper.

When the last roper is off the rope, the HRST master tells the aircraft commander "*Last man off rope*" and "*Rope being pulled to the 6 o'clock* (or whichever was briefed) *position*" or "*Rope retrieved.*"

UH-1N and H-60 Rappel

To execute a rappel from a UH-1N or H-60—

Load on command from the crew chief and inspect the installation of the rappel rope.

Ropers sit in their prebriefed positions.

Don your gunner's belt and perform an ICS check.

"*ICS check.*"

Once the aircraft commander responds, the HRST master acknowledges "*I have you loud and clear*" or "*I have you the same*" or "*I have you weak.*"

Once all ropers are seated and strapped in, the HRST master notifies the crew chief that "*Ropers are ready.*"

The crew chief clears the aircraft commander for departure.

After takeoff, the ropers remain strapped in and the HRST master remains oriented through periodic updates from the aircraft commander.

Once the aircraft commander gives the "*2-minute*" time warning, the HRST master responds, "*Roger, 2 minutes.*"

The HRST master holds up two fingers and each roper holds up two fingers on each gloved hand to indicate the "*2 minute*" command.

The HRST master ensures that each roper has his helmet, eye protection, and gloves and is ready to go.

Note: At no time will the HRST master leave an open rope station unattended.

The aircraft commander gives the "*1-minute*" call.

The HRST master responds, "*Roger, 1 minute.*"

The HRST master gives the "*1-minute*" command to the ropers using hand-and-arm signals.

Ropers make final checks of all gear.

Once the helicopter is in a stable hover, the aircraft commander gives the command "*Deploy the rope.*"

When the HRST master can see the target directly below, he responds, "*Roger, deploy the rope.*"

Once the helicopter is in a stable hover and the HRST master can see the target directly below, he deploys the rope.

The HRST master verifies that the rope is unfouled, on the deck, and on target, then he tells the aircraft commander "*Rope on the deck.*"

The HRST master connects a rappel rope to the roper before he unbuckles.

The HRST master uses hand-and-arm signals to command a roper to "*Unbuckle*" and "*Take position*" at the edge of the door opening. These commands are directed to one roper. All others remain seated and strapped in until told to unbuckle and take position.

The HRST master ensures that he has physical control of the roper to prevent loss of balance and falling out of the helicopter. The HRST master maintains this control until the roper is sent out and begins his descent down the rope.

The HRST master hooks the roper into the system, tells the aircraft commander, "*First man on rope*," physically controls the roper to the edge of the door opening, and verifies that the belay man is set (unless a self-belay system is being used).

The HRST master uses hand-and-arm signals to direct the roper to assume the L-shaped position over the edge and continues giving the roper the L position signal until he is ready to send him.

The HRST master gives the roper the "*Go*" hand-and-arm signal.

The roper pushes out and descends from the helicopter and starts his rappel.

The HRST master monitors the roper all the way to the deck.

Continue on with remaining ropers.

The HRST master ensures that after each roper is on the deck the belay man is reset before sending out the next roper.

When the last roper is off the rope, the HRST master tells the aircraft commander "*Last man off rope*" and "*Rope being pulled to the 3 or 9 o'clock* (whichever was briefed) *position*" or "*Rope retrieved.*"

Emergency Procedures

Emergencies can be encountered during rappelling operations. The following are guidelines to be used in the event of an emergency. However, due to adverse weather or other unusual conditions, modifications to these procedures may be required. Therefore, personnel must use sound judgment to determine the most appropriate course of action to be taken.

Helicopter Emergency

If the helicopter experiences engine failure or any other emergency while ropers are rappelling, ropers should descend as rapidly as possible and move from underneath the helicopter to the prebriefed position. The aircraft commander shall attempt to land the helicopter by moving forward.

In the event of a helicopter emergency, the HRST master shall—

- "*Abort*" (cease rope operations) on command from the aircraft commander.
- Ensure ropers already descending the rope are clear of the rope and possible helicopter impact area.
- Direct ropers still inside the helicopter to stay clear of openings, retake their seats, and "*Strap in*." All personnel shall then stand fast and await further instructions from the crew chief.

Unsafe Drift or Premature Lift Off

If the helicopter gains altitude so that the rope no longer touches the ground or if the helicopter drifts off target, the HRST must be halted until the helicopter is back on target or the helicopter's altitude is stabilized. The HRST master prebriefs Marines to brake if they have begun a descent and the helicopter begins to drift or change altitude. While ropers are rappelling, the HRST master stops ropers from starting a descent if the helicopter changes altitude or begins to drift. The HRST master may continue safe operations once the helicopter is back on target and/or altitude and approval is received from the aircraft commander.

Lost Communications/ICS Failure

In the event of an ICS failure, the following hand-and-arm signals apply:

- Abort (cease rope operations): a slashing motion of the right hand across the throat.
- Reposition the helicopter: an open palm moved in the direction required.
- Hold: a clenched fist (this means to stop the helicopter's movement or to brake [if directed at a roper]).
- Retake seats: point a finger toward the seats.
- Strap in: move both clinched fists together at the waist.

Hand-and-arm signals complete the descent of the roper on the rope. Rappelling operations cease while troubleshooting lost communications.

Rappelling operations resume once communications are restored.

Appendix C contains a list of hand-and-arm signals and their verbal commands.

Hung Roper

A roper who has exited the helicopter and is unable to complete his descent to the ground creates a potentially dangerous situation. The HRST master's first consideration is always the safety of the roper. A roper can become hung for a variety of reasons (e.g., fouled rope, loose clothing, straps, equipment, misplaced hand). In the event of a hung roper, the following steps are taken:

- The HRST master immediately notifies the aircraft commander.
- The aircraft commander lowers the roper to the ground until the hung roper's feet are on the deck. Once the hung roper's feet are on the ground or he is within 10 feet of the ground, the rope is cut. However, if the roper is hung more than 10 feet from the helicopter, he is assisted by the belay man and SIO to clear the rope.
- If the aircraft commander is unable to land and must search for a landing site, the HRST master ties a figure eight loop on the safety line, then attaches a steel locking carabiner. The safety line is secured to the inside of the helicopter at an anchor point opposite of the fouled rope's anchor points. The carabiner is then connected and lowered on the rappel ropes. The hung roper disconnects the safety carabiner from the rappel ropes and reconnects the safety carabiner and safety line to his seat carabiner.
- The aircraft commander is notified and the crew chief assists the HRST master.

- If the helicopter cannot descend, a safety line is rigged to establish a belay point. The safety line is rigged to the anchors opposite of the rappel station.
- To rig the belay, the HRST master ties a figure eight loop on one end of the safety line and attaches a steel locking carabiner. The safety line and steel locking carabiner are attached to the rappel ropes and lowered to the hung roper. The hung roper disconnects the safety line/carabiner from the rappel ropes and re-attaches them to his rappel seat. The HRST master secures the other end of the safety line with a suitable anchor knot to the anchor points opposite of the rappel system, leaving the last anchor point or the anchor closest to the ramp vacant. On this anchor point, the HRST master attaches a steel locking carabiner. The HRST master then uses a munter hitch to attach the safety line to the same carabiner that is hooked to the anchor point. The slack is removed from the safety line and the brake is applied. The rappeller is then instructed to free himself from the fouled rappel system.
- The HRST Master lowers the hung roper to the ground, releasing tension on the safety rope (belay).

Fouled Rope

A rope may become fouled or entangled on ground obstacles while rappelling. In the event of a fouled rope—

- Ensure all ropers are clear.
- If possible, descend or reposition helicopter over target to decrease tension on the rope.
- If sufficient tension cannot be released in order to release the rope, the aircraft commander may command, "*Cut rope.*"

CHAPTER 5
FAST ROPE OPERATIONS

Fast roping is a technique used to rapidly introduce heliborne personnel into areas that helicopters cannot land. Insertion via fast roping is preferred over rappelling due to its overall efficiency, effectiveness, and ease of installation. With proper familiarization and training, Marines can quickly acquire and retain the skill required to fast rope because this skill is less perishable than rappelling and requires less practice to remain proficient. The simplicity and speed of fast rope operations are its greatest attributes. However, fast roping does have a certain amount of risk since the roper is attached to the rope by only his hands and feet, and it is dangerous with heavy loads. This chapter establishes the basic guidelines for conducting fast roping operations and training Marines in the technique.

Familiarization

A thorough briefing is required for all users before fast rope operations are conducted. The brief should consist of, but not be restricted to, a review of all the equipment associated with fast rope, loading of personnel, helicopter approach, deplaning, descent, commands and signals, and preflight and in-flight safety procedures (see apps. A and B). For deplaning, it is essential that ropers receive the necessary training in fast rope techniques before using the fast rope on a tactical mission. When time and the situation permit, unqualified ropers may watch a fast rope operation or take part in the installation of equipment on the helicopter in order to familiarize the roper with both the equipment and fast rope techniques. Ropers unfamiliar with fast roping will initially conduct descents without combat equipment until confidence and skill level warrant more difficult operations.

Safety

When fast roping during a tactical operation, the benefit of safety verses tactical speed must be understood. Minimizing time over the target area reduces the inserting force's vulnerability to hostile fire. However, ropers unbuckling and standing at the ready prior to the helicopter decelerating, coming to a stable hover, and deploying the rope can be more dangerous to personnel than the length of time over the target. Prior to establishing a hover and deploying the rope, the aircraft commander may need to maneuver the helicopter to avoid an obstacle or take evasive action in response to a threat, which could place the roper in a potentially dangerous situation if he unbuckles prematurely. Therefore, proper unbuckling procedures must be followed. If tactical speed and faster insertions are necessary, they can be achieved through tower training, helicopter rehearsals, thorough briefings, and in-flight communications/situational awareness during the approach to the target.

Required Personnel and Equipment

The following is a list of personnel and equipment that is required during the conduct of fast rope training:

- One SIO.
- One HRST master per aircraft for the UH-1N and H-60 or one HRST master per rope station in the CH-46E, CH-53D/E, and H-47.
- One corpsman equipped with medical bag, cervical collar, and backboard with straps. The corpsman will not participate as a roper.
- One safety vehicle with driver. The driver will not participate as a roper.
- Radio communications with personnel in the insert zone.

Precautions

The following is a list of precautions that shall be adhered to during the conduct of fast rope training:

- A minimum of 10 feet of rope shall remain on the deck at all times to assist in stabilizing the running end of the rope.
- Ropers execute descents at speeds commensurate with their experience and proficiency in fast rope operations.
- The HRST master ensures that the tensile strength of the fast rope anchor points are not exceeded.
- During descent, ropers maintain visual contact with lower ropers and watch for obstructions.
- Individual ropers lock in during emergencies by standing on the fast rope with the other foot.
- Upon reaching the deck, ropers immediately run or roll out of the path of the next roper.
- The first roper on the deck may remain at the base of the rope and assist in keeping the rope steady for other ropers.
- A slight elastic reaction may be detected as a roper departs the rope.

The crew chief positions himself to observe the fast rope and assists in directing the aircraft commander in maintaining a stable hover over the target area. During descent, the helicopter may drift slightly causing the fast rope to hang at an angle vice vertical. If this occurs, the HRST master issues a *"Hold"* command until the crew chief directs the aircraft commander back over the target to restore a vertical rope position.

Anytime a fast rope is suspended from a helicopter, the HRST master or crew chief must be prepared to quickly release the rope if it becomes entangled with an object outside the helicopter.

During night fast rope, the use of multicolored chem lights is recommended to assist the HRST master in determining rope and roper positions. By attaching one chem light to the running end of the fast rope and one chem light 10 to 20 feet from the running end of the rope, the HRST master can determine when the rope is in contact with the ground and how much of the rope is on the ground. One chem light placed at the rope's standing end (anchor point) provides a reference for grabbing the rope. The HRST master can also wear a boot-banded chem light around his wrist to challenge/reply to the SIO and give the roper a reference for grabbing the rope. A small, firefly chem light attached to each roper illuminates each roper's position. Chem lights can also assist with hand-and-arm signals during night HRST operations. Chem lights are generally compatible with NVD use, but flashlights without the proper blue light lens are not.

Note: To avoid confusion, the SIO uses a different colored chem light than the one attached to the fast rope.

Rope Requirements

Rope Deployment

Only the aircraft commander authorizes deployment of the rope.

The helicopter must be in a stable hover prior to the "*Deploy the rope*" command.

Rope Retrieval

During non-tactical training evolutions, rope retrieval is accomplished from a hover or after the helicopter has landed. This can be accomplished by one of two methods. The first is to manually release the rope from the helicopter before the helicopter moves away to land. This method is used when immediate retrieval of the rope is not required. The second requires the ropers on the deck to hold the rope laterally so that it is clear of the rotors as the helicopter lands.

Restrictions

It is mandatory that the following restrictions be followed in order to avoid injury to personnel and damage to the helicopter.

UH-1N

- Only the gantry assembly configured with the original base plate is authorized for attachment of the fast rope.
- At no time shall the combined weight on the fast rope exceed 600 pounds.
- Dual and single gantry assemblies are optional for all fast rope operations. With the use of a single-fueled, auxiliary fuel cell, all fast roping must be conducted from the opposite side of the helicopter to ensure that the weight distribution does not exceed lateral limitations (i.e., one auxiliary fuel cell installed on the left side with a dual or single gantry assembly mounted on the right side).
- The gantry will be mounted at the forward port and/or starboard stations.
- During fast rope operations, the UH-1N's angle of pitch and roll must not exceed plus or minus 10 degrees.
- Gantry operations require that the forward wing doors be removed.

CH-46E

- The Schlomer frame can suspend two fast ropes simultaneously, but two ropes at once is unsafe due to the congested nature of the ramp area. Therefore, single rope operations are used from the Schlomer frame. The maximum weight capability of the Schlomer frame is 1,500 pounds.
- Fast rope operations that use the externally-mounted rescue hoist and boom as a fast rope attachment point are prohibited. However, hell hole operations can be accomplished using the fast rope interface kit. The maximum weight capacity during hell hole operations is 600 pounds.

CH-53D/E

- Due to the limitation of the quick disconnect pin assembly associated with the CH-53D fast rope anchor bar, at no time shall the combined weight placed on the release assembly exceed 600 pounds.
- Fast rope operations utilizing the externally-mounted rescue hoist and boom as a fast rope attachment point are prohibited.

H-47

- Only three ropers are authorized on any rope at any one time unless restricted by aircraft squadron standing operating procedures (SOPs).

H-60

- Only three ropers are authorized on any rope at any one time unless restricted by aircraft squadron SOPs.
- At no time should the total load placed on the rescue hoist exceed 600 pounds.
- Only the eye spliced fast rope may be used with the H-60 fast rope bar.

Rigging

All attaching systems incorporate a fail-safe rope quick release device. Due to the loads placed on attachment points during fast rope operations, careful inspection of helicopter rigging is mandatory by the HRST master and the aircraft commander to preclude injury to ropers and damage to the helicopter. Fast roping can be conducted from the UH-1N, CH-46E, CH-53D/E, H-47, and H-60 helicopters. Rigging the H-47 and H-60 helicopters may use equipment that is not organic to the Marine Corps. The gear in these procedures is organic to the aircraft assets that may be provided by the other Services.

Rigging the UH-1N

The simplistic design and lightweight structural composition of the gantry and base plate assembly allow for easy installation and removal, to include installation of safety belts on the cabin floor and safety straps on the overhead.

The UH-1N gantry assembly attaches to a vertical post with an extended link arm. The base plate must be secured to the cabin floor by two mounting studs (hard points) that share the fore and aft forces applied through the link arm. The top of the assembly is secured with a lock nut. All attachment points must be double checked for security to ensure personnel safety. The gantry assembly is not interchangeable from the right to left mounting positions due to the attachment of the link arm assembly. There is a right gantry assembly and a left gantry assembly and these should be properly marked and in place. The gantry assembly can be locked in two positions: inboard for stowage and extended outboard for operational use. The post can be manually rotated by unpinning the link arm to allow for repositioning of the boom assembly. The boom has a quick disconnect pin designed for the attachment of the fast rope and secondary safety. The fast rope is attached to the gantry through the bottom orifice of the gantry arm with a quick disconnect pin.

Rigging the CH-46E

Schlomer Frame

The Schlomer frame fits on the outside of the helicopter's conveyer roller guides located on the deck of the cargo ramp. It attaches to the helicopter at two forward and two aft mount points (see fig. 5-1). Each forward mount point consists of a bracket assembly that affixes to two floor tie down rings with ¾-inch quick disconnect pins. The aft mount points consist of two piano-hinged steel plates that slide into the same mount channels used for the vehicle loading extension panels. These panels must be removed in order to install the fast rope frame. The rope is attached to the frame at a U-section cross bar with a ¾-inch quick disconnect pin. The frame design enables the helicopter to fly with its ramp and hatch closed and the folded frame mounted and secured in place. When directed, the crew chief raises the hatch and lowers the ramp to a level position. With the aid of the HRST master, the crew chief unfolds the frame and locks the cross bar into place by inserting two ³∕₈-inch steel pins into the alignment holes. This pin alignment, insertion, and locking procedure is more difficult during night operations.

One person can accomplish the ramp/hatch configuration and the unfolding and deployment of the frame and rope. However, it is best performed jointly by the crew chief and HRST master.

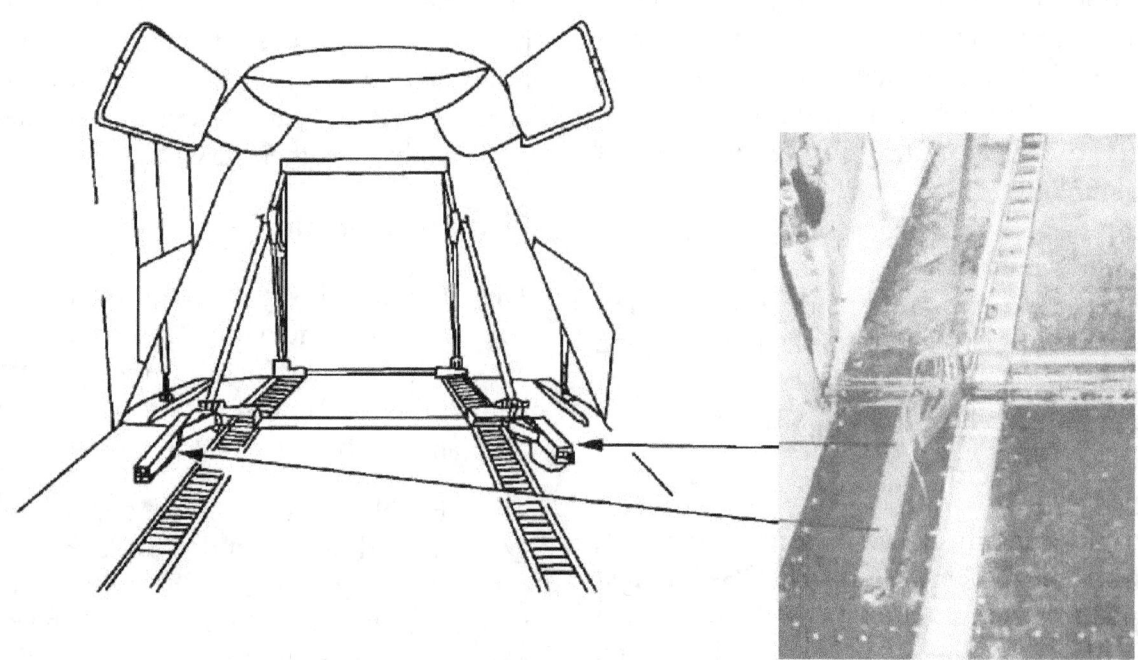

Figure 5-1. Schlomer Frame Installed.

Hell Hole

To prepare the helicopter for fast rope operations from the hell hole:

- Remove the cargo hook.
- Ensure there is a functional ICS and gunner's belt positioned near the hell hole.
- Ensure the seats on the HRST master's side of the hell hole are secured in the up position.
- Place all remaining seats in the locked down position.
- Attach a steel locking carabiner to the rescue pulley attachment structure above the hell hole.
- Attach a double clevis connector to the carabiner. The carabiner is locked with the locking nut running downward to lock.
- Fast rope head cap assembly ring is attached to the double clevis with a quick disconnect pin. The quick disconnect pin handle should be facing the HRST master. See figure 5-2.

Rigging the CH-53D

The CH-53D fast rope anchor bar secures to two brackets located on each cabin bulkhead at fuselage station 631.5, just aft of the ramp. The anchor bar can be easily removed when not in use.

To attach the fast rope, secure the fast rope head cap assembly ring to the quick release mechanism.

Two release assemblies are mounted on the anchor bar, 15 inches from each end. Each consists of a quick release mechanism that provides an anchor point for the fast rope (see fig. 5-3 on p. 5-6).

To jettison a rope, the quick release pins are removed from the quick release mechanisms, and the quick release arms are pushed simultaneously.

Rigging the CH-53E

The CH-53E A-frame fast rope attachment bar is manufactured by the MALS and maintained by the squadron. Prior to use, the HRST master inspects the bar for proper installation and

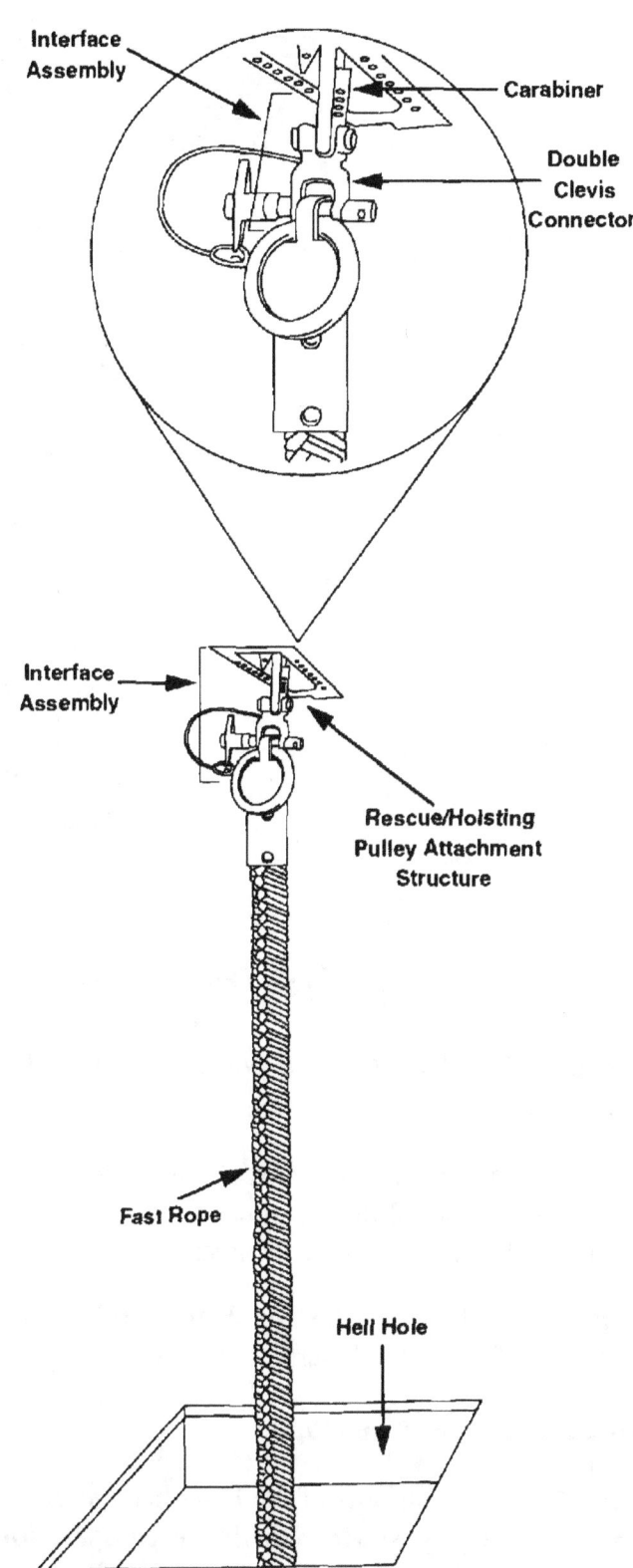

Figure 5-2. Fast Rope Interface Kit.

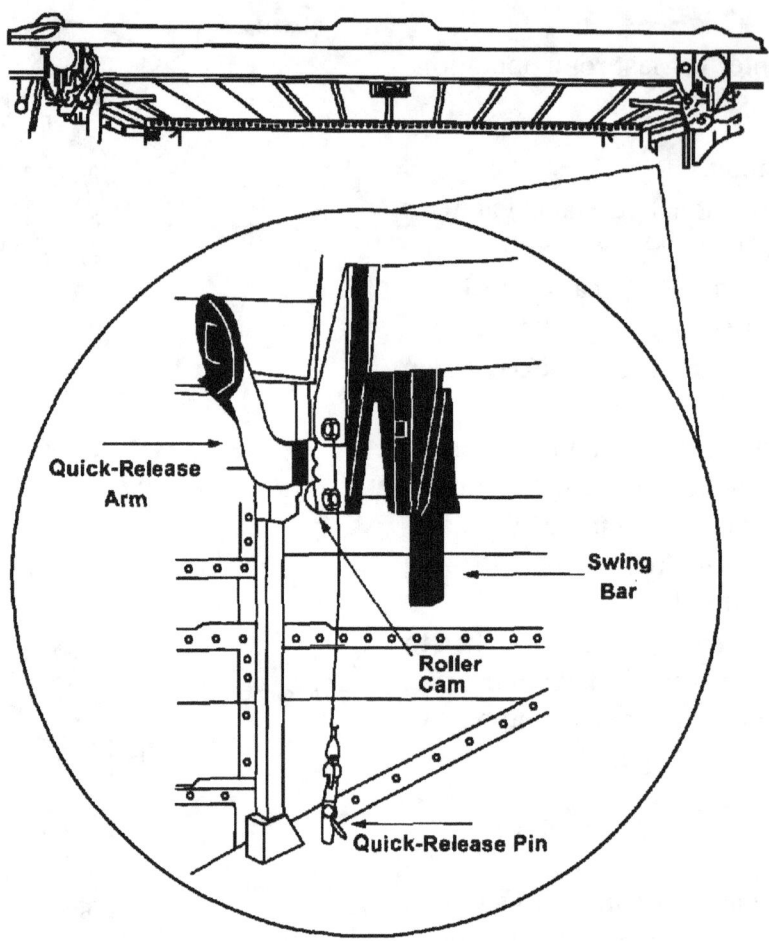

Figure 5-3. Fast Rope Anchor Bar and Quick Release Mechanism.

ensures that the nuts are present on each end of the bar and secured in place.

To attach the rope, the fast rope head cap assembly ring is secured to the 1-inch quick-release pin of the A-frame fast rope attachment bar assembly.

To jettison the rope, the 1-inch quick-release pin on the A-frame attachment bar is pulled.

Rigging the H-47 Helicopter

There are two variants of the H-47 helicopter that may be used by Marines for fast rope operation. The US Army flies both variants, which are the CH-47 and the MH-47.

Rope Stations

The two rope stations to support H-47 fast rope operations are the crew door and the ramp. Both stations utilize a Fast Rope Insertion Extraction System (FRIES) bar.

Ramp and Crew Door Station

Both the ramp and the crew door stations utilize the FRIES bar for hookup of the fast rope. The aircraft squadron is responsible for the installation and setup of the FRIES bar. When using an eye-spliced fast rope, the HRST master must use a fabricated aluminum sleeve (see fig. 5-4) with the quick-release pin. This eliminates the risk of the quick-release pin causing an indentation in the woven loop of the fast rope and making it difficult to release. The following procedures outline the setup of the fast rope with the H-47 FRIES bar:

- Insert the fast rope eye splice (with sleeve) or the fast rope metal ring into the attachment bracket.
- Insert the quick-release pin and secure with a cotter pin.
- Attach the safety line to the FRIES bar or another secondary strong point using a double clevis and quick-release pin.
- Tape or secure any excess safety line so that it does not interfere with the fast rope operation.
- Pad and tape any sharp edges.

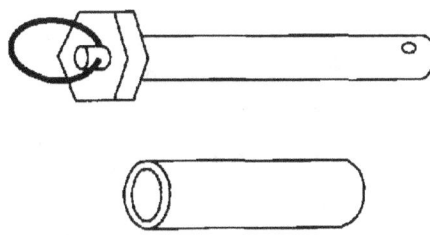

Figure 5-4. FRIES Quick-Release Pin and Fabricated Aluminum Sleeve.

Rigging the H-60 Helicopter

There are four variants of the H-60 helicopter that may be used by Marines. The single door HH-60 and SH-60 are flown by the US Navy. The HH-60 is also flown by the US Coast Guard. The double door UH-60 is flown by the US Army. The double door MH-60 is flown by AFSOC.

Rope Stations

The two rope stations to support H-60 fast rope operations are the rescue hoist and the fast rope bar. The UH-60 and MH-60 utilize the fast rope bar and can be configured for both doors. The HH-60 and SH-60 utilize the rescue hoist and are configured for single door only (see fig. 5-5). Some HH-60/SH-60 squadrons are also equipped with the fast rope bar.

Rescue Hoist Station (HH-60/SH-60)

The following procedures are used in rigging the H-60 rescue hoist station for fast rope operations:

- Place the fast rope end cap (or G-12 clevis for eye spliced rope) inside the double clevis link and insert the quick-release pin.

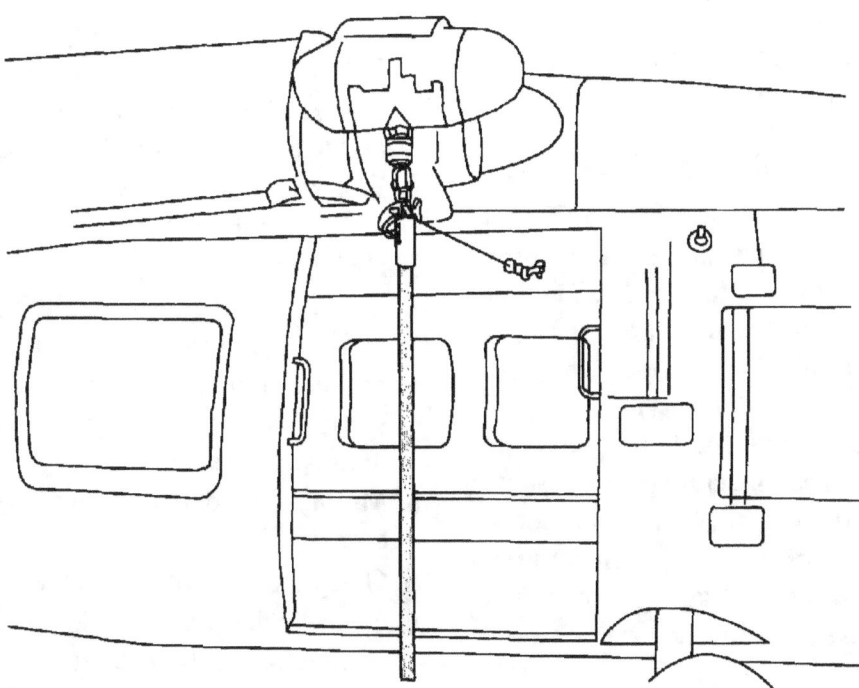

Figure 5-5. SH-60 Shown Rigged for Fast Rope Using Rescue Hoist.

- Attach the double clevis, using a 10K locking carabiner, to the large retrieval hook of the rescue hoist. Hook gate latch must close fully.
- Ensure brake of recovery winch is set.
- Route safety line up toward recovery hoist, along coupling or eye splice. Tape safety line while routing to prevent line from becoming entangled. Continue routing through small retrieval hook.
- Attach safety line to overhead red tie down ring (see fig. 5-6) using a carabiner and double clevis with quick-release pin.

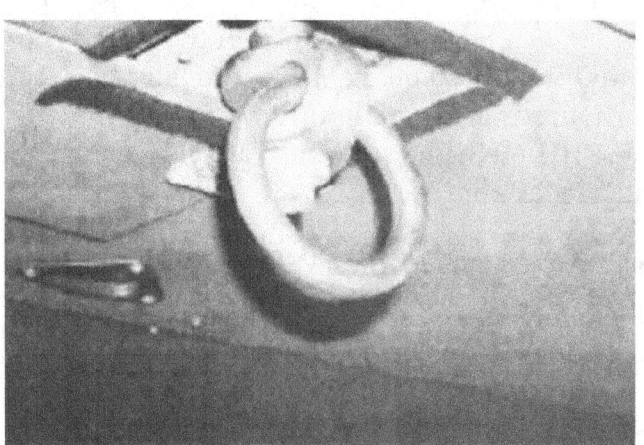

**Figure 5-6. H-60 Overhead
Red Tie Down Ring.**

- Pad or tape all sharp edges of aircraft door and ensure door is locked open.

Fast Rope Bar Station (MH-60/UH-60 some HH-60).

The fast rope bar, sometimes called the FRIES bar, is a hardware system that is mounted in the overhead of the aircraft using four bolts. The bar is installed by the aircraft squadron and designed for quick installation of the fast rope. Only the eye-spliced fast rope may be used with the H-60 fast rope bar. Fast ropes with hardware end caps interfere with the fast rope bar release pin. Seats in the aircraft are removed to allow more room for the fast ropers. Floor restraints are provided when the seats are removed. Rigging procedures for the fast rope bar are as follows:

- Lock door in the open position.
- Extend the fast rope bar and insert pin to lock.

- Inspect the bar for cracks or damage.
- Ensure release cables are attached and release handles are securely mounted.
- Check function of releases:
  o With latch closed and downward pressure on release arm, latch SHOULD NOT open when release is pulled.
  o With latch closed and no pressure applied, latch SHOULD open when release is pulled.
  o With latch closed and safety pin installed, latch SHOULD NOT open when release is pulled.
- Install fast rope onto bar and insert locking pin.
- Route safety line up towards bar, along eye splice. Tape safety line while routing to prevent line from becoming entangled.
- Attach safety line to overhead tie down ring or secondary anchor point using a carabiner and double clevis with quick release pin.
- Pad or tape all sharp edges of aircraft near door.

Roper Responsibilities

Ropers must—

- Understand and comply with all aspects of HRST and emergency procedures.
- Ensure all safety equipment is properly donned and inspected by an HRST master.
- Ensure seat belts are hooked up prior to take off and unbuckled only on command by the HRST master.
- Maintain eye contact with the HRST master at all times prior to grabbing the rope.
- Make deliberate movements toward the rope station while maintaining a hand hold in the helicopter at all times.
- Mount the rope only on the HRST master's command.
- Grasp the rope firmly. Never jump for the rope.
- Control descent speeds and brake to avoid landing on another roper or injuring yourself.
- Look down at the deck and the roper below you while descending.

● Move rapidly away from the rope upon landing. If you are unsteady upon landing or if you fall, immediately roll to your side and away from the rope to prevent injury from follow-on ropers.

Sequence of Events

Note: HRST master's ICS calls are in bold italic.

CH-46E, CH-53D, CH-53D/E Hell Hole, and H-47 Ramp/Crew Door Fast Rope

To execute fast roping from the CH-46E, CH-53D, CH-53D/E hell hole, or H-47 ramp/crew door—

Load on signal from the crew chief. Ropers sit down and buckle in.

The HRST master inspects installation of the fast rope.

The HRST master dons a gunner's belt and performs an ICS check.

"ICS check."

Once the aircraft commander acknowledges the ICS check, the HRST master responds, *"I have you loud and clear"* or *"I have you the same"* or *"I have you weak."*

Once ropers are seated and strapped in, the HRST master notifies the crew chief *"Ropers are ready."*

The crew chief clears the aircraft commander for departure.

After takeoff, the ropers remain strapped in, and the HRST master remains oriented through periodic updates from the aircraft commander.

Once the aircraft commander gives the "*2-minute*" warning, the HRST master responds, *"Roger, 2 minutes."*

The HRST master holds up two fingers and each roper holds up two fingers on each gloved hand to indicate the "*2-minute*" command.

The HRST master ensures that each roper has on his helmet, eye protection, and gloves and is ready to go.

For hell hole operations, the crew chief assists the HRST master by opening the hell hole door.

Note: At no time will the HRST master leave an open rope station unattended.

The aircraft commander gives the "*1-minute*" call.

The HRST master responds, *"Roger, 1 minute."*

The HRST master gives the "*1-minute*" command to the ropers using hand-and-arm signals.

Ropers perform final checks of all gear and give the "*1-minute*" signal.

Once the helicopter is in a stable hover and the target is directly below, the aircraft commander gives the command *"Deploy the rope."*

The HRST master responds, *"Roger, deploy the rope."*

When the mission dictates and it is verified that the rope is not fouled, on the deck, and on target, the HRST master tells the aircraft commander *"Rope on the deck."*

The HRST master uses hand-and-arm signals to command the ropers to "*Unbuckle*" and "*Take position.*"

The HRST master physically controls the roper to prevent loss of balance and falling out of the helicopter. This control is maintained until the roper begins his descent down the rope.

The HRST master is positioned on either side of the hell hole, beside the Schlomer frame, or to the side of the CH-53D or H-47 ramp.

To avoid confusion, the HRST master and the ropers should know the order of departure.

Ropers can feed into the hell hole from either direction (forward or aft).

Subsequent ropers continue to mount the rope.

Once the last man is on the deck, the HRST master informs the aircraft commander *"Last man on deck."*

The HRST master then informs the aircraft commander *"Rope being pulled to 6 o'clock* (or whichever was briefed) *position"* or *"Rope is jettisoned"* or *"Rope retrieved."*

UH-1N and H-60 Fast Rope

To execute fast roping from the UH-1N or H-60—

Load on signal from the crew chief. Ropers sit down and buckle in.

The HRST master inspects the installation of the fast rope.

Don your gunner's belt.

The HRST master calls for an "*ICS check.*"

Once the aircraft commander acknowledges the ICS check, the HRST master responds, "*I have you loud and clear*" or "*I have you the same*" or "*I have you weak.*"

Once ropers are seated and strapped in, the HRST master notifies the crew chief "*Ropers are ready.*"

The crew chief clears the aircraft commander for departure.

After takeoff, the ropers remain strapped in, and the HRST master remains oriented through periodic updates from the aircraft commander.

Once the aircraft commander gives the "*2-minute*" warning, the HRST master responds, "*Roger, 2 minutes.*"

The HRST master holds up two fingers and each roper holds up two fingers on each gloved hand to indicate the "*2-minute*" command.

The HRST master ensures that each roper has on his helmet, eye protection, and gloves and is ready to go.

Note: At no time will the HRST master leave an open rope station unattended.

The aircraft commander gives the "*1-minute*" call.

The HRST master responds, "*Roger, 1 minute.*"

The HRST master gives the "*1-minute*" command to the ropers using hand-and-arm signals.

Ropers execute final checks of all gear and give the "*1-minute*" signal.

Once the helicopter is in a stable hover and the target is directly below, the aircraft commander gives the command "*Deploy the rope.*"

The HRST master responds, "*Roger, deploy the rope.*"

When the mission dictates and it is verified that the rope is not fouled, on the deck, and on target, the HRST master tells the aircraft commander "*Rope on the deck.*"

The HRST master uses hand-and-arm signals to command the ropers to "*Unbuckle*" and "*Take position.*"

The HRST master physically controls the roper to prevent him from falling out of the helicopter once his lap belt has been removed. This control is maintained until the roper begins his descent down the rope.

To avoid confusion, the HRST master and the ropers should know the order of departure.

Subsequent ropers continue to mount the rope.

Once the last man is on the deck, the HRST master informs the aircraft commander "*Last man on deck.*"

The HRST master then informs the aircraft commander "*Rope being pulled to 3 or 9 o'clock* (or whichever was briefed) *position*" or "*Rope is jettisoned*" or "*Rope retrieved.*"

Emergency Procedures

Emergencies can be encountered during fast roping operations. The following are guidelines to be used in the event of an emergency. However, due to adverse weather or other unusual conditions, modifications to these procedures may be required. Therefore, personnel must use sound judgment to determine the most appropriate course of action to be taken.

Helicopter Emergency

If the helicopter experiences engine failure or any other emergency while fast roping, ropers should descend as rapidly as possible and move from beneath the helicopter to the prebriefed position. The aircraft commander shall attempt to land the helicopter by moving forward.

In the event of a helicopter emergency, the HRST master shall—

● "*Abort*" (cease rope operations) on command from the aircraft commander.

● Ensure ropers already descending the rope are clear of the rope and possible helicopter impact area.

● Direct ropers still inside the helicopter to stay clear of openings, retake their seats, and "*Strap in*." All personnel shall then stand fast and await further instructions from the crew chief.

Unsafe Drift or Premature Lift Off

If the helicopter gains altitude so that the rope no longer touches the ground or if the helicopter drifts off target, the HRST must be halted until the helicopter is back on target or the helicopter's altitude is stabilized. The HRST master prebriefs Marines to "*Lock in*" if they have begun a descent and the helicopter begins to drift or change altitude. While fast roping, the HRST master stops ropers from starting a descent if the helicopter changes altitude or begins to drift. The HRST master may continue safe operations once the helicopter is back on target and/or altitude and approval is received from the aircraft commander.

Lost Communications/ICS Failure

In the event of ICS failure, the following hand-and-arm signals apply:

● Abort (cease rope operations): a slashing motion of the right hand across the throat.

● Reposition the helicopter: an open palm moved in the direction required.

● Hold: a clenched fist (this means to stop the helicopter's movement or to brake [if directed at a roper]).

● Retake seats: point a finger toward the seats.

● Strap in: move both clinched fists together at the waist.

Hand-and-arm signals are used to complete the descent of the roper on the rope. Rappelling operations cease while troubleshooting lost communications. Rappelling operations resume once communications are restored.

Appendix C contains a list of hand-and-arm signals and their verbal commands.

Fouled Rope

A rope may become fouled or entangled on ground obstacles while fast roping. In the event of a fouled rope, execute the following steps:

● Ensure all ropers are clear.

● If possible, descend or reposition helicopter over target to decrease tension on the rope.

● Release the rope.

CHAPTER 6
SPECIAL PATROL INSERTION AND EXTRACTION OPERATIONS

The Special Patrol Insertion and Extraction (SPIE) system rapidly inserts/extracts a reconnaissance patrol from an area that does not permit a helicopter landing. During SPIE operations, the SPIE rope is lowered into the pickup area from a hovering helicopter and patrol personnel hook up to the SPIE rope. The helicopter lifts vertically from the extract zone until the rope and personnel are clear of obstructions, then proceeds in forward flight to a secure insert zone. The rope and personnel are treated as an external load; therefore, airspeeds, altitudes, and oscillations must be monitored. This chapter establishes the basic guidelines for conducting SPIE operations and training Marines in the technique.

Familiarization

All personnel should participate in familiarization training prior to conducting SPIE operations. Familiarization should consist of, but not be limited to the following procedures: SPIE safety, donning individual equipment, mounting, in-flight, emergency, and dismounting. All individuals training in SPIE for the first time conduct extracts without combat equipment. This assists in building the ropers' confidence levels.

Safety

All operations using the SPIE system are preceded by a safety brief. The safety brief should consist of, but not be limited to, a review of all the equipment associated with the SPIE system, its characteristics, extraction and insertion methods, and, most importantly, emergency procedures (see apps. A and B). The following safety measures are taken during SPIE operations.

Required Personnel and Equipment

The following is a list of personnel and equipment that is required during the conduct of SPIE training:

- One SIO.
- One HRST master per aircraft.
- One corpsman equipped with medical bag, cervical collar, and backboard with straps (the corpsman will not participate as a roper).
- One safety vehicle with driver (the driver will not participate as a roper).
- Radio communications with personnel in the insert zone.

Communications

The distance between the ropers tethered on the SPIE rope, the HRST master's location inside the helicopter, and helicopter noise make voice communications impossible. During the pre-flight brief to HRST participants, hand-and-arm signals between ropers and the HRST master are covered in detail and must be clearly understood by all HRST members.

Airspeed

Airspeed shall not exceed 70 knots in warm weather operations or 50 knots during cold weather operations.

Altitude

A minimum clearance of 100 feet from the lowest roper on the line to the highest obstacle on the deck must be maintained for SPIE operations prior to transitioning to forward flight during extract and beginning the descent during insert. The aircrew uses the helicopter's radar altimeter to maintain a safe altitude for ropers. The radar altimeter's reading when the last roper is lifted off of the deck is used to determine obstacle clearance and assists in insert of ropers into the next zone. During insert, the helicopter should not descend faster than 300 feet per minute.

Hell Hole

The hatch is open during CH-46E and CH-53D/E SPIE operations, therefore, care must be taken to avoid an accidental fall-through while working around the hell hole.

Rigging/Donning Equipment

SPIE can be conducted from the UH-1N, CH-46E, CH-53D/E, and H-60 helicopters.

Rigging the UH-1N

Primary Method

Four 9-foot cargo slings and four Type IV connectors may be used to rig the UH-1N SPIE system and create a back-up sling assembly. To rig the UH-1N—

- Connect two cargo slings end-to end to constitute one "loop" through the helicopter. A second set of two cargo slings are also connected end-to-end to constitute a second loop.
- Both loops must pass above the skids and through the eye of the SPIE rope. The slings must be kept as far aft as possible so not to alter the helicopter's center of gravity and degrade aircraft handling. Two of the Type IV connectors must be inside the helicopter.
- When using this method, eight carabiners are required to connect the slings to eight different cargo tie downs, four carabiners per loop (see fig. 6-1).

Alternate Method

In the alternate method of rigging the UH-1N, the primary attachment point for the SPIE rope is the cargo hook. To rig the UH-1N—

- Attach the polyurethane encapsulated eye end of the SPIE rope to the cargo hook.

Note: It is important that the aircraft commander disengage the cargo hook release so that an accidental release does not occur.

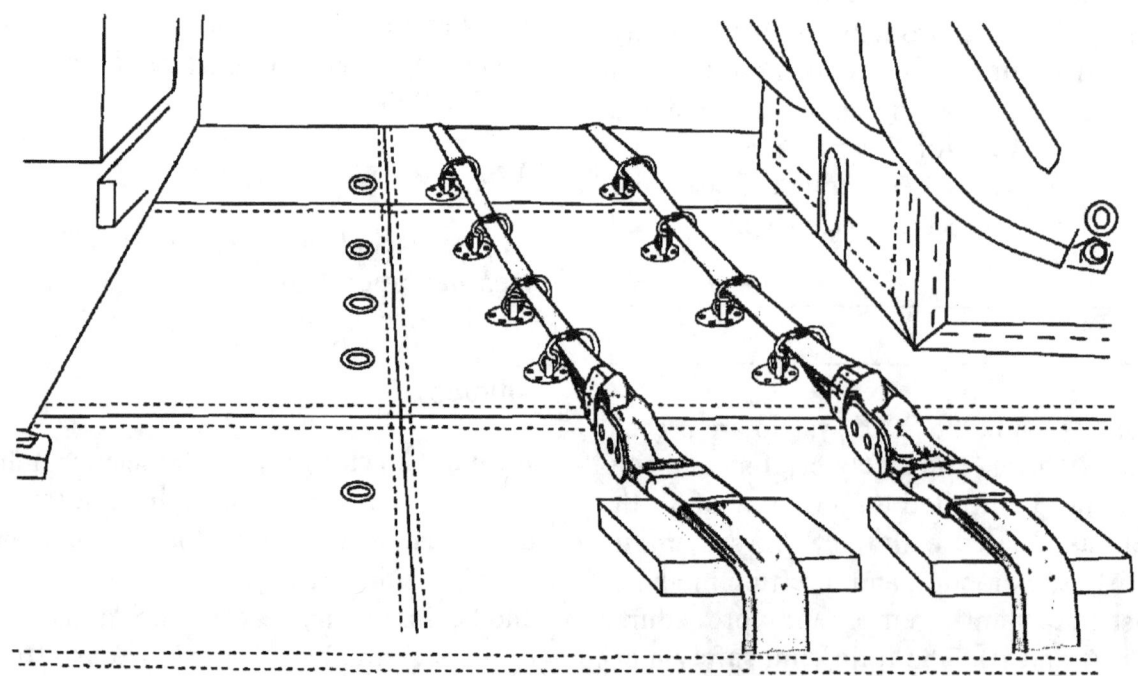

Figure 6-1. Primary Installation.

- Use a Type IV connector to join the two 9-foot cargo suspension slings together to form one continuous sling.
- Stretch the sling out on the helicopter deck.
- Take one end of the sling under the helicopter and through the eye of the SPIE rope and con-

nect it to the other end of the sling using a Type-IV connector assembly (see fig. 6-2).

Note: The sling must pass between the helicopter skids and the fuselage.

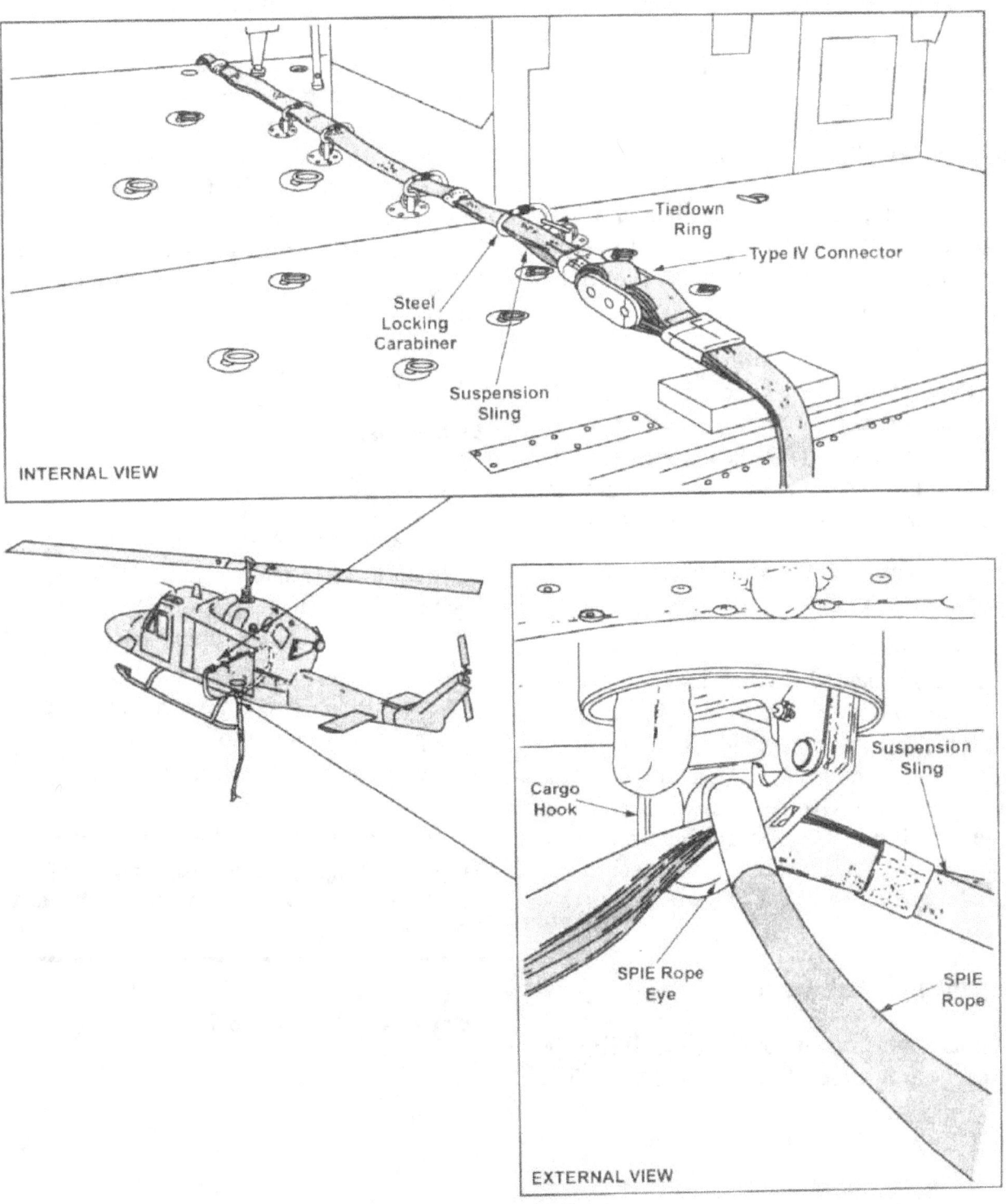

Figure 6-2. Alternate Intallation.

- Use locally procured padding to protect the sling from damage.
- Once the SPIE rope and cargo slings are in place, use at least four, and as many as eight, locking carabiners to secure the straps that are across the deck of the helicopter in place.
- Space carabiners evenly across the deck, in line with the gates facing up, locked and away from the anchor point. Each carabiner encompasses the top two straps.

Rigging the CH-46E and CH-53D/E

Installed properly, the cargo straps hold the SPIE rope comfortably in the center of and slightly below the opening of the cargo hatch. To rig the CH-46E and CH-53D/E—

- Use two 9-foot cargo suspension slings and four Type IV connectors to attach the SPIE rope to the aircraft.
- Pass cargo slings through the encapsulated eye of the SPIE rope and attach it to the outboard cargo tie down rings on the helicopter floor.

Note: The cargo slings run forward and aft not port and starboard.

- Use two tie down rings for each cargo sling.
- Use locally procured padding around the edge of the hell hole to protect slings from damage.
- Attach locking carabiners close to all tie down points to create a backup in case of a faulty tie down ring. This also reduces the amount of movement in the cargo straps. Use a total of eight locking carabiners, two at each point (linked together), with the gates facing up (see fig. 6-3).

Rigging the H-60 Helicopter

The primary attachment point for the SPIE rope is the cargo hook (see fig. 6-4 on p 6-6). The polyurethane encapsulated eye end of the SPIE rope is attached to the cargo hook. Cargo slings are used as a safety in case the primary hookup fails. One 9-foot cargo suspension sling is routed through the overhead tie down rings. A 10K carabiner is attached to each end of the 9-foot sling. The large end of a double clevis link with quick release pin is then attached to each carabiner (see fig. 6-5 on pg. 6-6). Ensure the gates are locked on the carabiners. A second 3-foot cargo sling is routed through the eye of the SPIE rope and connected to the free end of each double clevis using 10K carabiners (see fig. 6-6 pg 6-6). This forms one continuous safety loop through the cargo hatch. Locally procured padding may be used around the edge of the cargo hatch to protect slings from damage.

Donning Equipment

SPIE Harness

To don the SPIE harness—

- Pass arms through shoulder loops.
- Route the free end of the chest strap through chest adapter making sure that the strap is back laced through the chest adapter for a quick release system.
- Attach the V-ring of each leg strap to the respective ejector snap.
- Tighten chest and leg straps to a snug fit.

────────────── WARNING ──────────────

To prevent injury during use, ensure that harness chest and leg straps are adjusted to a snug fit.

────────────────────────────────────

See figure 6-7 on page 6-7.

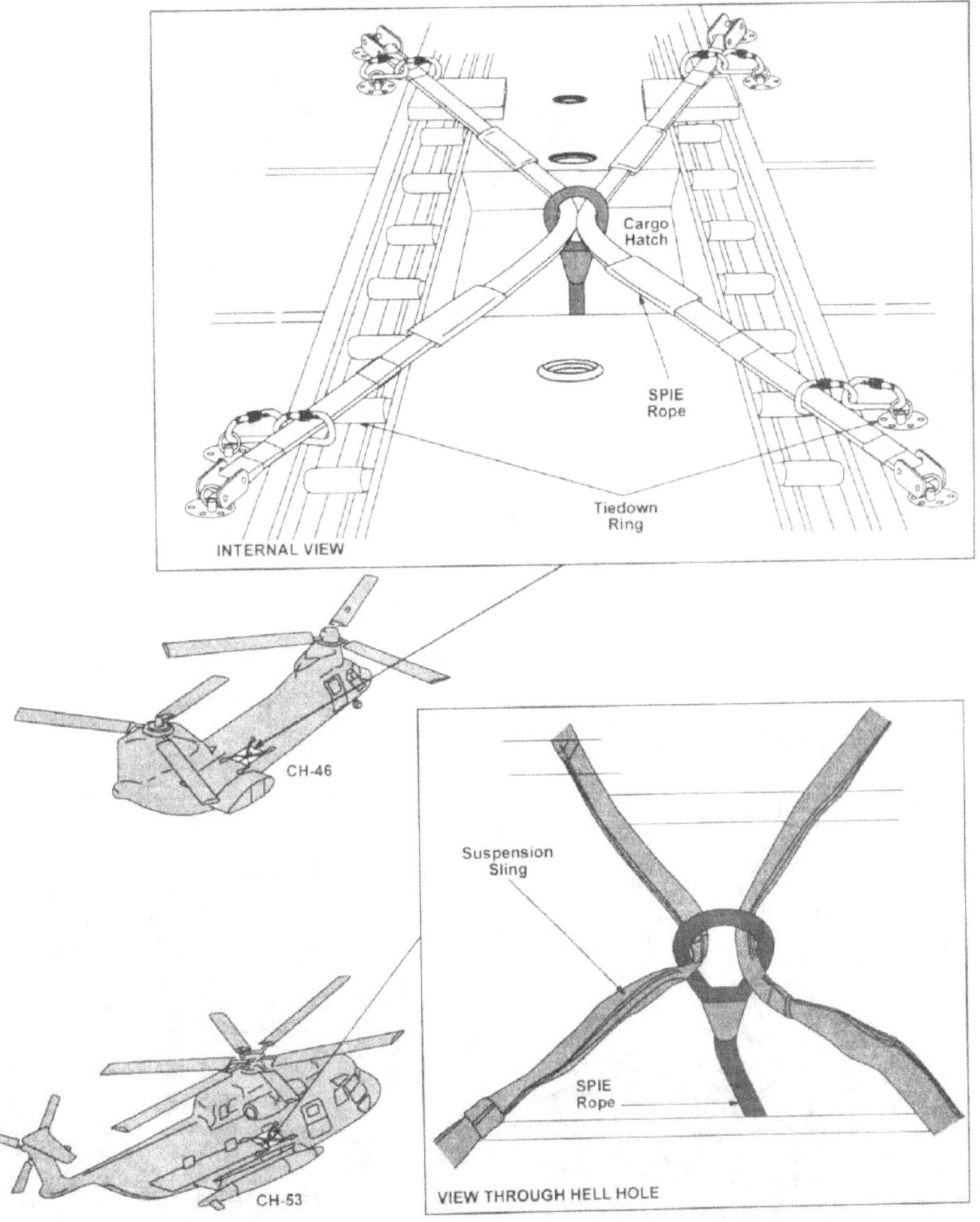

Figure 6-3. CH-46E and CH-53D/E SPIE Rope Installation.

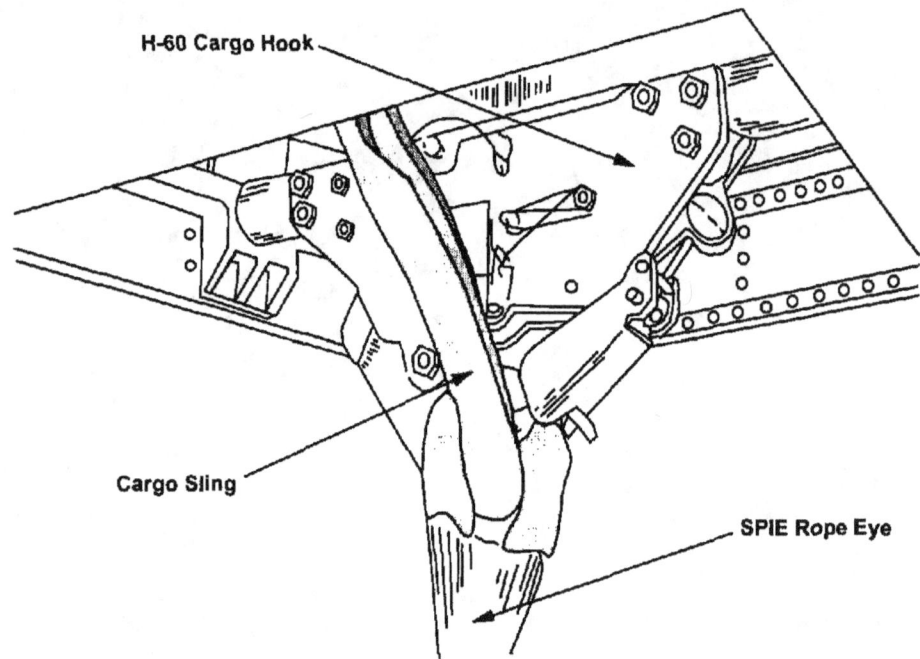

Figure 6-4. Cargo Hook.

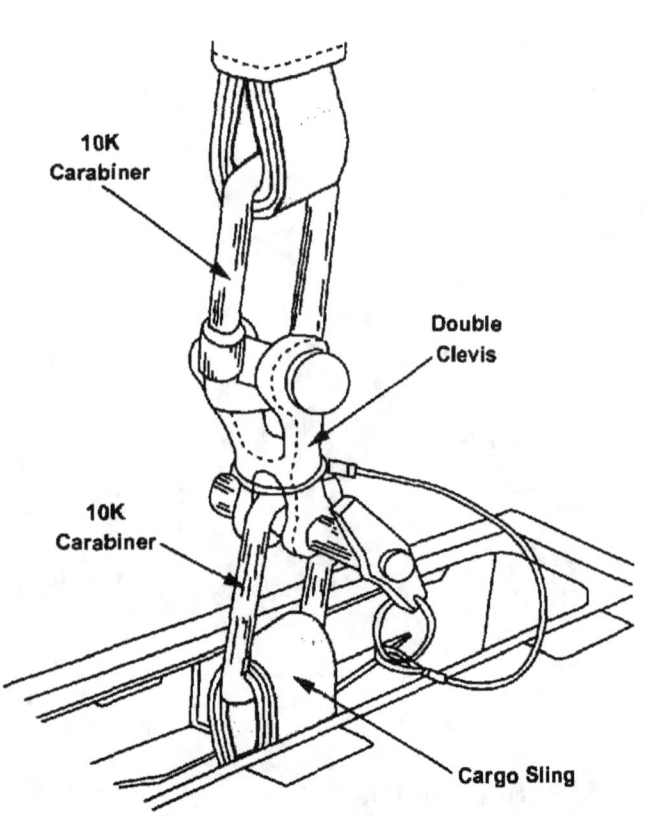

Figure 6-5. Double Clevis Hook Up.

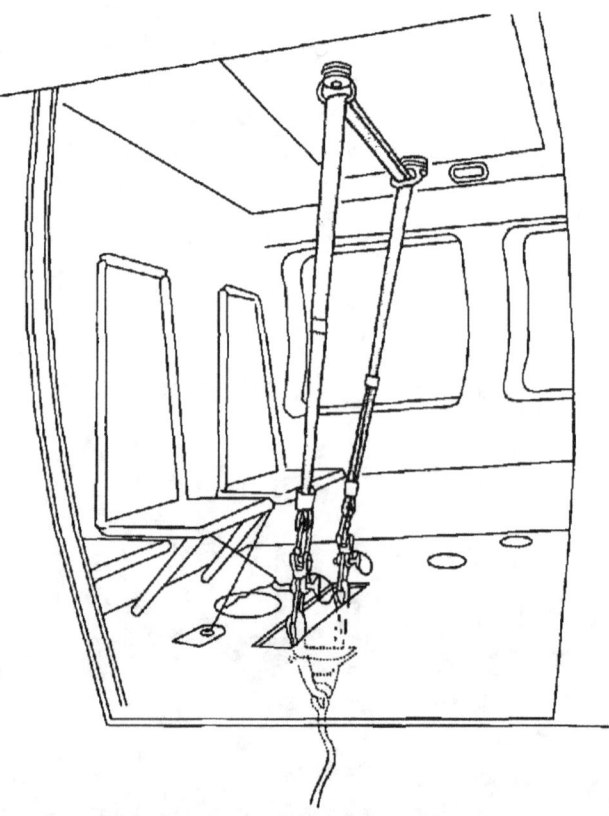

**Figure 6-6. H-60 Rigged with
the SPIE Rope and Safety Sling.**

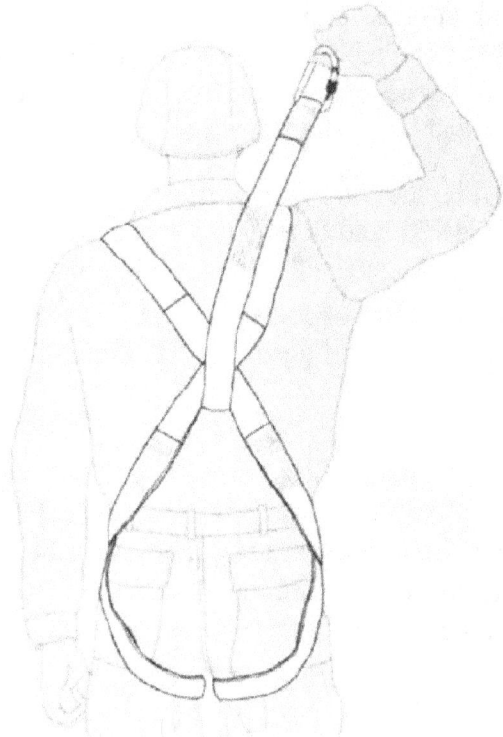

Figure 6-7. SPIE Harness.

Safety Line

A sling rope is used to make a safety line. A safety line for normal attachment of the carabiner on the D-ring consists of the 12- to 15-foot sling rope and an additional carabiner. The rope is secured around the roper's chest with a bowline knot. The roper then takes the running end of the sling rope and extends it to arms length. A figure eight loop is made and a carabiner is then connected to the upper or lower D-ring of the SPIE rope. Do not attach the carabiner to the same D-ring as the harness. The backup attachment is intended for use in training exercises and is worn under the SPIE harness (see fig. 6-8).

Roper's Responsibilities

Training and safety equipment decrease the inherent dangers of SPIE operations—it does not

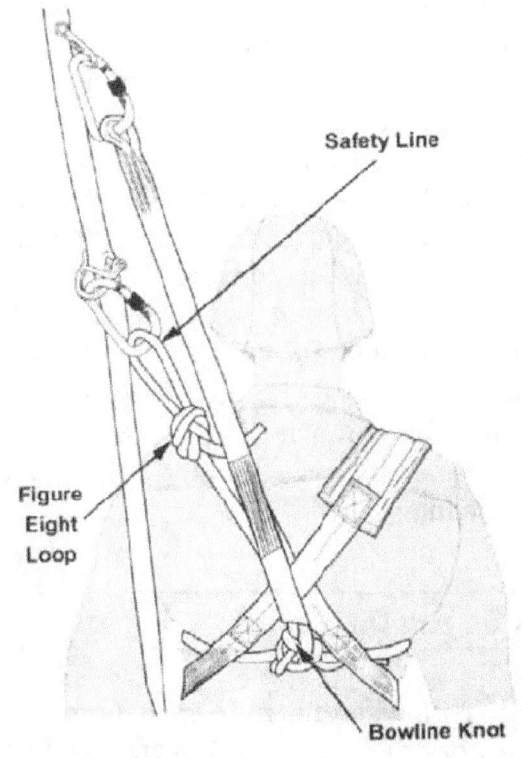

Figure 6-8. Safety Line.

eliminate the dangers. SPIE safety depends largely upon the technical expertise and prudent judgment of the individual SPIE roper. Ropers are responsible for the following:

- Understanding and complying with all aspects of HRST and emergency procedures.
- Ensuring that all safety equipment is properly donned and inspected by a HRST master.
- Properly donning the SPIE harness, ensuring a snug fit.
- Inspecting the safety line.
- Maintaining periodic eye contact with the HRST master during extraction, flight, and descent if you are the uppermost roper.
- Repeating all commands issued by the HRST master through the top roper.
- Mounting the rope only after it has contacted the deck.
- Maintaining eye contact with the deck while descending.
- Moving out from under higher ropers immediately upon contacting the deck.
- Moving to the appropriate pre-briefed position (3, 9, or 12 o'clock) once on the deck.
- Ensuring that during training the primary and secondary anchor devices are not disconnected until the helicopter is sitting on the deck to avoid fingers being injured in a carabiner. If the helicopter is not going to land, ropers disconnect the primary and secondary anchor devices only after their feet touch the deck.
- Remaining prepared to disconnect any injured or unconscious ropers.
- Moving rapidly away from the SPIE rope upon dismounting.

Hook Up and Dismounting

Roper positions on the rope are determined and assigned prior to mounting. Ropers may be positioned as singles, pairs, or any combination as long as the rope's bottom point is always filled.

Load the line starting from the bottom positions and then move to the top positions.

To execute a single hook up—

- Place your safety line and main lift web over your shoulder closest to the rope.
- Approach the rope on the proper side from the running end of the rope.
- Attach primary lift web carabiner to the D-ring closest to the helicopter and secure the gate.
- Attach your secondary carabiner to the D-ring on the opposite side of the rope, to the farthest D-ring from the helicopter and secure the gate.
- Place the main lift web, safety rope, and SPIE rope over the top of your inboard shoulder and give the thumbs up signal with your outboard hand to signify that you are ready to lift.

To execute pair hook up, each roper—

- Places his safety line and main lift web over his shoulder closest to the rope.
- Attaches his main lift web carabiner to D-ring on his side of the rope and his safety carabiner to his partner's primary attachment D-ring and secures the gates.

Note: Ensure all carabiners are attached to a D-ring, not another carabiner.

- Partners hold each other around the waist, ensuring all ropes and main lift webs pass over the top of the shoulders, and give the thumbs up signal to signifying they are ready to lift. As the helicopter begins to ascend, begin walking toward the helicopter. The idea is to be located directly under the helicopter when all slack is removed from the rope. As you start to lift, let go of the SPIE rope but maintain "thumbs up" throughout the initial ascent until everyone is airborne, and the helicopter transitions to forward flight.
- Once suspended from the rope, keep your arms extended to reduce the spinning. Do not adjust your harness in any way. Should your helmet feel like it is coming loose, grasp it by the conscript to hold it in place.

To execute water hook up—

- Three inflatable life vests or flotation devices are tied to the SPIE rope to provide buoyancy for the rope while in the water. Tie one flotation device at each end of the attachment points and one flotation device at each end of the attachment point area, just above the middle two sets of D-rings. The reconnaissance swimmers wear SPIE harnesses under their life vests. They may also wear swimming fins, a mask, and a snorkel to facilitate hook up to the SPIE rope within the spray area beneath the hovering helicopter.

- After the extraction helicopter attains a stable hover 50 to 70 meters away from the reconnaissance swimmer's location, the HRST master lowers the SPIE line hand-over-hand, with flotation attached, on order from the aircraft commander. The aircraft commander maneuvers the helicopter in order to drag the line to the swimmers.

_____ **Caution** _____

During initial lift off, team members may be dragged through the water; therefore, they should be prepared to roll on their backs until they are clear of the water.

To dismount—

- When the extraction helicopter has reached a safe dismount area, a transition is made to a hover 100 feet above the highest obstacle from the lowest roper on the line.

_____ **Caution** _____

High hovers are more difficult due to lack of references and can result in excessive descent rates and/or drift.

- Once the helicopter is clear of all obstacles a vertical descent is commenced.
- The aircrew and HRST master provide continuous altitude and clearance information to the aircraft commander.

Upon reaching the deck, all ropers should immediately head in the direction of the helicopter's 3 or 9 o'clock position for the CH-46 and CH-53 or the 12 o'clock position for the UH-1 and H-60. If the helicopter is making a scheduled landing at this time, it will be up to the team to ensure that the rope is pulled taut to the 3, 9, or 12 o'clock position respectively as the helicopter descends vertically to land.

Note: If landing on a ship or on an oil platform, team members take orders from the deck personnel in charge of the landing platform the moment they step on the deck.

During training and if the helicopter is going to land, your primary and secondary anchor devices are not disconnected until the helicopter is sitting on the deck to avoid injury to fingers in a carabiner. During tactical evolutions and when the helicopter is not going to land, primary and secondary anchor devices are disconnected after the roper's feet touch the deck. Once on the deck, ropers immediately begin walking in the direction stated during the roper's brief. Be cautious not to drag fallen ropers or to pull the rope so tight that it binds on the edge of the helicopter. Keep walking away from the helicopter until all ropers are on the deck.

Sequence of Events

Note: HRST master's ICS calls are in bold italic.

CH-46E and CH-53D/E SPIE

To execute SPIE operations from the CH-46E and CH-53D/E—

Load on command from the crew chief and install/inspect the installation of the SPIE rope.

The HRST master dons a gunner's belt and performs an ICS check.

**"ICS check."**

Once the aircraft commander responds, the HRST master acknowledges, "*I have you loud and clear*" or "*I have you the same*" or "*I have you weak*."

The HRST master notifies the crew chief once he is ready "*HRST master all set.*"

The crew chief clears the aircraft commander for departure.

As the helicopter moves to the extract zone, the aircraft commander gives the HRST master time warnings per briefing guidelines. At a minimum, the aircraft commander gives the HRST master a "*1-minute*" warning.

At the "*1-minute*" warning, the HRST master responds by saying "*Roger, 1-minute.*"

The HRST master takes position on the forward side of the hell hole.

Once the helicopter is over the extract zone, the aircraft commander commands, "*Clear to deploy rope.*"

The HRST master responds, "*Roger, deploy rope,*" and deploys the SPIE rope through the hell hole.

Once the rope is deployed and on the deck, the HRST master notifies the aircraft commander "*Rope is on the deck.*"

————— **Caution** —————

Ensure the rope is deployed through the proper opening of the type-26 cargo slings so as not to create a twist in the installation. Twists in the installation can degrade the load bearing capacity of the rig.

The extract team begins to hook up.

The HRST master tells the aircraft commander "*Ropers hooking up.*"

Once all ropers are hooked up, the team leader gives the HRST master a two thumbs up signal.

The HRST master notifies the crew chief that "*Ropers are ready.*"

The crew chief clears the aircraft commander for lift.

As the helicopter begins to lift, the HRST master monitors the ropers for any emergency and the team leader for the hold signal.

The aircraft commander lifts the helicopter straight up and begins ascent, correcting any drift immediately.

If ropers are pulled into trees, the best course of action is to continue lift. If the ropers become hopelessly entangled, the HRST master may have to cut the rope. If the rope must be cut, the aircraft commander must command, "*Cut rope, cut rope, cut rope.*" Once the rope is clear, the HRST master tells the aircraft commander "*Rope jettisoned.*"

If extracting off of an elevated platform (e.g., rooftop, oil platform) and the ropers become entangled, the helicopter must continue its ascent. If corrections must be made for drift, the helicopter continues its ascent as it is making its drift corrections. Otherwise the ropers may fall over the edge causing serious injury and possible death.

At approximately 85 feet above ground level (AGL), the top roper(s) become airborne. Once the top roper is airborne, the HRST master tells the aircraft commander "*First man off the deck.*"

At approximately 120 feet AGL, the bottom roper(s) become airborne. The HRST master notifies the aircraft commander by saying "*Last man off the deck.*"

The aircraft commander continues to ascend the helicopter straight up, calling out his altitude. When he calls out an altitude of 250 feet AGL or higher, the HRST master says, "*Ready for forward flight.*" At this time the crew chief ensures that the helicopter and ropers are clear of all obstacles and clears the aircraft commander for forward flight.

Throughout the flight, the HRST master monitors the ropers for any emergency signal. Periodically, the HRST master informs the aircraft commander that, "*Ropers look good.*" If a problem occurs, the HRST master informs the aircraft commander, "*Sir, we have a problem on the rope. We need to put the ropers down immediately.*" The aircraft commander proceeds to the nearest/pre-briefed landing zone.

As the helicopter comes over the landing zone, the crew chief talks the aircraft commander into a steady hover at a minimum altitude of 250 feet AGL.

Once stabilized in a hover, the aircraft commander begins the helicopter's descent.

The crew chief advises the aircraft commander of the lowest ropers' distance above the deck.

When the bottom roper reaches the deck, the HRST master tells the aircraft commander "*First man on deck.*"

When the top roper reaches the deck, the HRST master tells the aircraft commander "*Last man on deck.*"

As each roper reaches the deck, he moves in a pre-briefed direction (3 or 9 o'clock).

Once the last roper reaches the deck, the HRST master tells the aircraft commander the direction the ropers are moving "*Ropers moving to your 3 o'clock.*"

At this point, the crew chief takes over and clears the aircraft commander to land the helicopter.

——————— **Caution** ———————

Ensure the aircraft commander does not land the helicopter on the SPIE rope, as this will damage the rope.

UH-1N and H-60 SPIE

SPIE operations are performed as follows for the UH-1N and H-60:

Note: An end-of-the-line prussic must be attached to the SPIE rope just below the encapsulated eye and then anchored to an anchor point inside the helicopter. This is how the SPIE is retrieved in the event the rope must be pulled back into the helicopter.

Load on command from the crew chief and inspect the installation of the SPIE rope.

The HRST master dons a gunner's belt and performs an ICS check.

"*ICS check.*"

Once the aircraft commander responds, the HRST master acknowledges, "*I have you loud and clear*" or "*I have you the same*" or "*I have you weak.*"

The HRST master notifies the crew chief once he is ready "*HRST master all set.*"

The crew chief clears the aircraft commander for departure.

As the helicopter moves to the extract zone, the aircraft commander gives the HRST master time warnings per the briefing guidelines.

At a minimum, the aircraft commander gives the HRST master a "*1-minute*" warning.

At the "*1-minute*" warning, the HRST master responds by saying "*Roger, 1 minute.*"

The HRST master lies across the helicopter cabin with his head on the same side as the chopping block.

Once the helicopter is over the extract zone, the aircraft commander commands "*Clear to deploy rope.*"

The HRST master responds, "*Roger, deploy rope,*" and deploys the SPIE rope between the skid and the fuselage.

Once the rope is deployed and on the deck, the HRST master notifies the aircraft commander "*Rope is on the deck.*"

Once all ropers are connected to the SPIE rope, and the SIO gives a double thumbs up to the HRST master, the HRST master notifies the crew chief that "*Ropers are ready.*"

The crew chief clears the aircraft commander for helicopter lift.

The crew chief immediately provides drift corrections to the aircraft commander as the helicopter lifts straight up.

At approximately 85 feet AGL, the top roper(s) become airborne. The HRST master tells the aircraft commander "*First man off the deck.*"

At approximately 120 feet AGL, the bottom roper(s) become airborne. The HRST master notifies the aircraft commander by saying "*Last man off the deck.*"

The aircraft commander continues to ascend the helicopter straight up, calling out his altitude.

Once the HRST master hears an altitude of 250 feet AGL or higher, he says, "*Request forward flight.*" At this time the crew chief ensures that the helicopter and ropers are clear of all obstacles and clears the aircraft commander for forward flight.

Throughout the flight, the HRST master monitors the ropers for any emergency. Periodically, the HRST master informs the aircraft commander that, "*Ropers look good*" if no problems exist. If a problem occurs, the HRST master informs the aircraft commander, "*Sir, we have a problem on the rope. We need to put the ropers down immediately.*" The aircraft commander proceeds to the nearest/pre-briefed landing zone.

As the helicopter comes over the landing zone, the crew chief talks the aircraft commander into a steady hover at a minimum altitude of 250 feet AGL.

Once stabilized in a hover, the aircraft commander begins the helicopter's descent.

The crew chief advises the aircraft commander of the lowest ropers' distance above the deck.

When the bottom roper reaches the deck, the HRST master tells the aircraft commander "*First man on deck.*"

When the top roper reaches the deck, the HRST master tells the aircraft commander "*Last man on deck.*"

Once the ropers have reached the deck, they pull the rope out to the 12 o'clock position so as not to damage the helicopter's nose-mounted, forward-looking infrared pod.

Once the last man reaches the deck, the HRST master tells the aircraft commander the direction the ropers are moving, "*Ropers moving to your 12 o'clock*".

At this point, the crew chief takes over and clears the aircraft commander to land the helicopter.

——————— **Caution** ———————

Be aware of the wire cutter mounted on the nose of the helicopter as this could damage the rope should it come in contact with it.

Emergency Procedures

Emergencies can be encountered during SPIE operations. The following are guidelines to be used in the event of an emergency. However, due to adverse weather, or other unusual conditions, modifications to these procedures may be required. Therefore, personnel must use sound judgment to determine the most appropriate course of action to be taken.

Aircraft Emergency

If the helicopter experiences engine failure or other aircraft emergency during operations, ropers on the ground must rapidly move from beneath the helicopter to the pre-briefed position. The aircraft commander attempts to land the helicopter by moving forward.

Hung Roper

The roper or any other participant may give the emergency signal. When one roper gives the signal, all ropers give the signal until the situation is corrected. During daylight operations, the emergency signal is given by placing both hands on top of the helmet. During night operations, ropers will initiate the pre-briefed emergency signal.

Fouled Rope

A rope may become fouled or entangled on ground obstacles while conducting SPIE operations. In the event of a fouled rope, execute the following steps:

- Ensure all ropers are clear.
- If possible, descend or reposition helicopter over target to decrease tension on the rope.
- Release the rope.
- If sufficient tension cannot be released in order to release the rope, the aircraft commander may command "*Cut rope.*"

CHAPTER 7
JACOB'S LADDER OPERATIONS

Like the SPIE system, Jacob's ladder operations were developed as a means to rapidly extract personnel from an area that does not permit a helicopter landing. Unlike SPIE operations, Jacob's ladder does not require that a special harness be worn by personnel being extracted. Ladder operations are suitable for land, water, and waterborne extractions. In water extractions, personnel mount the ladder directly from the water. In waterborne extractions, personnel mount the ladder from boats, barges, and oil platforms. This chapter establishes the basic guidelines for employing Jacob's ladder and training Marines in the techniques needed to conduct a successful operation using the Jacob's ladder.

Familiarization

Personnel should demonstrate the ability to climb a Jacob's ladder prior to attempting to do it from a helicopter. All personnel (HRST master, climbers, and aircrew) must have performed a day of ladder recovery training before conducting a night ladder recovery.

Safety

All operations using Jacob's ladder are preceded by a safety brief. The safety brief should consist of, but not be limited to, a review of all the equipment associated with the Jacob's ladder, its characteristics, extraction and insertion methods, and, most importantly, emergency procedures (see apps. A and B).

Required Personnel and Equipment

The following is a list of personnel and equipment that is required during the conduct of Jacob's ladder training:

Land ladder operations:
- One SIO.
- One HRST master.
- One safety vehicle and driver.
- One corpsman with medical bag, cervical collar, and backboard with straps.
- Radio communications with personnel in the pick up zone.

Water or waterborne ladder operations:
- One SIO afloat.
- One HRST master.
- Two safety boats and coxswains.
- Two water survival qualified safety swimmers, one per safety boat.
- One safety vehicle and driver ashore.
- Two corpsman, one ashore with medical bag, cervical collar and backboard with straps, and one afloat.
- Two radio communicators, one ashore and one afloat.

Rigging

Jacob's ladder can be adapted to a variety of helicopters. To rig Jacob's ladder use the following procedures:

- Roll the ladder onto itself, starting from the running end, leaving the starting end exposed and available for rigging.

- Attach the port tubular nylon anchor device to a cargo tie down ring using two steel locking carabiners.
- Attach the starboard tubular nylon anchor device to a cargo tie down ring using two steel locking carabiners.
- Lock all four carabiners.
- Place a wooden block under each anchor line just aft of the anchor point. In the event of an emergency in which the aircraft commander directs, "*Cut rope*" the blocks allow the rope cutting device to cut completely through the anchor lines, releasing the ladder.
- Pad and tape all areas where the Jacob's ladder comes in contact with the edge of the ramp. Ensure the area of the ladder and recovery position in the aircraft are free of any grease or oil.

As with all HRST operations, the HRST master requires an ICS headset and a gunner's belt.

Note: In the CH-46E, the Jacob's ladder may be rigged with the fast rope Schlomer frame in place to provide additional handholds for the HRST master and climbers during extraction.

Climber Responsibilities

Climbers are responsible for the following:

- Understanding and complying with all safety and emergency procedures.
- Immediately upon entering the aircraft, being seated and fastening seat belts.
- Unfastening seat belt only upon the direction of the HRST master or crew chief.
- Maintaining periodic eye contact with the HRST master prior to and throughout ascent.
- Never allowing more than two climbers on the ladder at one time.

Sequence of Events

Note: HRST master's ICS calls are in bold italic.

To execute Jacob's ladder operations—

The HRST master rigs the aircraft and conducts an aircrew safety brief in accordance with appendix A.

The HRST master prepares the ladder for deployment, ensuring the emergency rope cutting device is easily accessible.

The HRST master performs an ICS check. *"ICS check."*

Once the aircraft commander responds, the HRST master acknowledges, *"I have you loud and clear"* or *"I have you the same"* or *"I have you weak."*

The HRST master notifies the crew chief once he is ready, *"HRST master all set."*

Upon reaching the predetermined contact point, the aircraft commander attempts to establish radio communications with the extract personnel.

Upon contact, the aircraft commander maneuvers the helicopter to the extract point.

The aircraft commander passes the *"1 minute"* advisory to allow the crew chief and HRST master to prepare for deployment of the ladder. The HRST master responds by saying *"Roger, 1 minute."*

The HRST master unbuckles his seatbelt, dons his gunner's belt, and positions himself to deploy the ladder.

The crew chief, with the assistance from the HRST master, provides guidance to the aircraft commander in positioning the helicopter over the extraction site.

The aircraft commander clears the HRST master to *"Deploy the ladder."*

The HRST master rolls the ladder off the ramp and then advises the aircraft commander *"Ladder out."*

Caution is exercised when deploying the ladder to avoid striking climbers below.

Climbers must avoid contact with the ladder until it touches the surface and discharges static electricity.

The HRST master advises the aircraft commander "*Climber #____ inside*" as the climbers enter the helicopter. The first climber grasps the ladder with one arm and reaches over the ladder with the opposite arm, grasping the opposite side of the ladder. The climber moves up the ladder until his feet are out of the water. He waits to continue his climb until the next climber has grasped the ladder. This helps hold the ladder vertically for the next climber. Climbers should grasp the stringers and not the rungs to prevent the higher climber from stepping on their hands. The crew chief directs the climbers to strap in. After the last climber enters the helicopter, the aircraft commander directs the HRST master to release or retrieve the ladder.

Note: The ladder should be retrieved during multiple training evolutions, rather than jettisoned.

——————— **Caution** ———————

Do not allow the helicopter to transition to forward flight with the ladder deployed. The ladder could get caught on an obstacle resulting in damage to the helicopter and embarked passengers.

The HRST master retrieves the ladder into the helicopter using a hand-over-hand method, fan folding it onto itself. The HRST master informs the aircraft commander "*Ladder clear.*"

The crew chief confirms to the aircraft commander that the ladder is retrieved and the aircraft is clear of all obstacles. Once assured that all is clear, the aircraft commander transitions the helicopter to forward flight or lands during multiple training evolutions.

To execute a night recovery—

The aircrew wears NVDs as directed by current policy. Climbers will not wear NVDs during the recovery because of difficulties with depth perception.

The HRST master uses chem lights to aid in the visual signals when conducting night operations. For night training evolutions, all personnel should have chem

lights rigged to their helmets or forearms for easy identification. The HRST master should also have lights to identify his position in the aircraft.

The Jacob's ladder has chem lights at both anchor points and on each side of the ladder on every other step. This aids personnel in grasping the ladder during recovery.

The HRST master can rig a weighted line with two different colored chem lights to aid in determining the altitude of the helicopter. The HRST master knows the helicopter is at the proper altitude when the bottom light is not visible and the top one is visible. If both lights are visible, then the helicopter altitude is too high.

All lighting used in the operation must be compatible with the aircrew's NVDs.

Emergency Procedures

The HRST master and the climbers must be prepared to address aircraft emergencies. Multiple emergencies, adverse weather, or other unusual conditions my require modifications to these procedures. Therefore, personnel must use sound judgment to determine the most appropriate course of action to be taken.

Aircraft Emergency

If the helicopter experiences engine failure or other aircraft emergency during operations, climbers on the ladder must descend as rapidly as possible and move from beneath the helicopter to the pre-briefed position. The aircraft commander attempts to land the helicopter by moving forward. Upon notification by the aircraft commander of an emergency, the HRST master—

- Signals the climbers already inside the aircraft to "*Abort*" and "*Strap in.*" Once seated and secured, all personnel then follow the directions of the crew chief.
- Ensures that climbers already ascending the ladder complete the climb and enter the helicopter. Personnel on the surface must stay clear of the ladder and possible helicopter impact area.

Hung Climber

A hung climber is a climber who has begun his ascent and is unable to complete it. A climber can become hung for a variety of reasons: fouled clothing, straps, equipment. In the event of a hung climber, initiate the following procedures:

- Immediately notify the aircraft commander.
- If possible, the aircraft commander lowers the climber to the surface.
- If the aircraft commander is unable to land and must search for a landing site, lower a safety line with a steel locking carabiner down the ladder to the hung climber. The hung climber connects the safety line to himself using the carabiner. The HRST master secures the safety line to a cargo tie down ring.

Fouled Ladder

A ladder may become fouled or entangled on obstacles during the course of ladder operations. In the event of a fouled ladder, initiate the following procedures:

- Immediately notify the aircraft commander of the fouling.
- Ensure all climbers are clear.
- If possible, the aircraft commander descends or repositions the aircraft in order to decrease tension on the ladder.
- Release the three anchor points and allow the ladder to fall to the ground.
- As a last ditch effort to free a fouled ladder, the aircraft commander can give the, "*Cut Rope*" command. The HRST master cuts the anchor lines and allows the ladder to fall to the surface.

Unsafe Drift or Premature Lift Off

If the helicopter gains altitude so that the ladder no longer touches the ground/water or if the helicopter drifts off target, the HRST must be halted until the helicopter is back on target or the helicopter's altitude is stabilized. The HRST master may continue safe operations once the helicopter is back on target and/or altitude and approval is received from the aircraft commander.

Appendix A
HRST Mission Briefs to HRST Participants

This appendix provides the mission briefs used by the HRST master to brief participants on the operating area, individual actions and responsibilities, safety precautions, and emergency procedures prior to conducting HRST operations. The mission briefs in this appendix include—

- Tower rappel.
- Tower fast rope.
- Helicopter rappel.
- Helicopter fast rope.
- Helicopter SPIE.
- Jacob's ladder.

TOWER RAPPEL BRIEF

1. Hold muster.

2. General operations information.

    a. HRST master.

    b. SIO.

    c. Area for HRST operations.

    d. Type of HRST and method to be used.

    e. Location of safety vehicle.

    f. Location of corpsman.

    g. Other personnel.

3. HRST preparation.

    a. Personnel.

        (1) Corpsman.

        (2) Drivers.

        (3) Working party.

    b. Formation time.

    c. Type of transportation.

    d. HRST time.

    e. Safety checks (HRST master/assistant HRST master).

4. HRST training area (map).

5. Actions in the staging area.

    a. Muster.

    b. Equipment and safety check.

    c. Review HRST commands/hand-and-arm signals.

6. Actions on the tower.

    a. Watch for HRST master's signals.

    b. Watch the HRST master for hook up directions.

(1) Hold brake hand out to grasp rappel line.

(2) Put on brake while moving to exit point.

    (a) Assume "L" position.

    (b) "Go" on signal.

7. Actions on rappel.

  a. Keep good body position.

  b. Make at least three brakes during descent.

8. Actions on the deck.

  a. Belay man moves to the roper's front and grasps the rope.

  b. Roper backs up, not stepping on the rope, holds the rope to his rear with his brake hand, and places his left hand above the carabiner to prevent the rope from snapping up into his face.

  c. Once clear, roper performs a side straddle hop while sounding off that he is off the rappel.

  d. Roper moves to the assembly area.

9. Malfunctions.

  a. If the roper becomes hung and cannot complete the rappel, the HRST master lowers a safety line with a carabiner down the rappel line to the hung roper. The hung roper connects the safety line to his rappel seat hard point using the carabiner. The HRST master lowers the hung roper to the deck.

  b. If the roper's hands slip off the rope, the belay man puts tension on the rope and stops the ropers descent and slowly lowers the roper to the deck.

10. Belay man.

  a. Watch the roper, if he gets out of control or loses his grip on the rope, immediately take action to slow/stop his rappel.

  b. Maintain control of the running end of the rope by holding the running end around your body and be prepared to put a braking action on the rope.

  c. Give the roper enough slack so not to interfere with his brake.

  d. Gloves are not worn while belaying.

TOWER FAST ROPE BRIEF

1. Hold muster.

2. General operations information.

    a. HRST master.

    b. SIO.

    c. Area for HRST operations.

    d. Type of HRST and method to be used.

    e. Location of safety vehicle.

    f. Location of corpsman.

    g. Other personnel.

3. HRST preparation.

    a. Personnel.

        (1) Corpsman.

        (2) Drivers.

        (3) Working party.

    b. Formation time.

    c. Type of transportation.

    d. HRST time.

    e. Safety checks (HRST master/assistant HRST master).

4. HRST training area (map).

5. Actions in the staging area.

    a. Muster.

    b. Equipment and safety check.

    c. Review HRST commands/hand-and-arm signals.

6. Actions on the tower.

    a. Watch for HRST master's signals.

    b. HRST master taps only the first roper off the tower.

7. Actions on the fast rope.

   a. Maintain eye contact with the HRST master at all times prior to beginning a descent.

   b. Make deliberate movements toward the rope station.

   c. Grasp the rope upon command from the HRST master.

   d. Grasp ropes firmly (never jump for the rope).

   e. Control descent speeds and brake two-thirds of the distance down to avoid landing on another roper or injuring yourself.

   f. Look down at the deck and the roper below you while descending.

   g. Spread feet shoulder-width apart when you are 3 to 5 feet from the deck and prepare to land.

8. Actions on the deck.

   a. Move rapidly away from the rope upon landing. If you are unsteady upon landing or if you fall, immediately roll to your side and away from the rope to prevent injury from following ropers.

   b. Move to the assembly area.

9. Malfunctions.

   If the roper becomes hung and cannot complete the fast rope, the HRST master reaches over the edge of the tower and pulls the hung roper back up onto the tower.

HELICOPTER RAPPEL BRIEF

1. Hold muster and prepare a passenger manifest.

2. General operations information.

    a. HRST master.

    b. SIO.

    c. Area for HRST operations.

    d. Type of HRST and method to be used.

    e. Type of helicopter.

    f. Total number of ropers to exit.

    g. Location of rope station(s) in the aircraft.

    h. Location of safety vehicle.

    i. Location of corpsman.

    j. Other personnel.

3. HRST preparation.

    a. Personnel.

        (1) Corpsman.

        (2) Drivers.

        (3) Working party.

    b. Formation time.

    c. Type of transportation.

    d. HRST time.

    e. Number of sticks.

    f. Number of operations.

    g. Exit sequence, by name.

    h. Safety checks (HRST master/assistant HRST master).

4. HRST training area.

    a. Location (map).

    b. Aerial photograph.

    c. Obstacles on/near HRST training area.

    d. Flight plan.

    e. Exit point.

5. Actions in the loading area.

    a. Muster.

    b. Equipment and safety check.

    c. Loading order and seating arrangement.

    d. Review HRST commands/hand-and-arm signals.

6. Actions in the helicopter.

    a. Secure seatbelts, unbuckle on HRST master's signal only.

    b. Watch for HRST master's signals.

    c. Watch HRST master for hook up directions.

        (1) Hold brake hand out to grasp rappel line.

        (2) Put on brake while moving to exit point.

            (a) Assume L position.

            (b) "*Go*" on signal.

7. Actions on rappel.

    a. Keep good body position.

    b. Make at least three brakes during descent while looking at the deck over the right shoulder.

8. Actions on the deck.

    a. Belay man moves to the roper's front and grasps the rope.

    b. Roper backs up, not stepping on the rope, holds the rope to his rear with his brake hand, and places his left hand above the carabiner to prevent the rope from snapping up into his face.

    c. Once clear, roper performs a side straddle hop.

    d. Roper moves to the assembly area.

9. Zone control.

    a. Radio call sign.

    b. Frequency/alternate frequency.

    c. Visual signals/air panels.

d. Radio check prior to operation.

e. Actions for radio failure.

10. Malfunctions.

    a. Hung roper.

        (1) The HRST master requests that the aircraft commander move the helicopter to a place where he can safely lower the hung roper to the deck. If the roper is hung just below the helicopter, the HRST master requests that the aircraft commander lower the helicopter to about 10 feet above the deck and the HRST master pulls the hung roper back inside the helicopter.

        (2) The HRST master lowers a safety line with a carabiner down the rappel line to the hung roper. The hung roper connects the safety line to his rappel seat hard point using the carabiner. The HRST master lowers the hung roper to the deck.

    b. Roper's hands slip off the rope.

        (1) Belay man puts tension on the rope and stops the roper's descent.

        (2) Belay man slowly lowers the roper to the deck.

11. Belay man.

    a. Watch the roper, if he gets out of control or loses his grip on the rope, immediately take action to slow/stop his rappel.

    b. Maintain control of the running end of the rope by holding the running end around your body and be prepared to put a braking action on the rope.

    c. Give the roper enough slack so not to interfere with his brake.

    d. If the helicopter has to descend, maintain a taut rope while backing away from the helicopter.

    e. Goggles are to be worn.

    f. Gloves are not worn while belaying.

HELICOPTER FAST ROPE BRIEF

1. Hold muster and prepare a passenger manifest.

2. General operations information.

    a. HRST master.

    b. SIO.

    c. Area for HRST operations.

    d. Type of HRST and method to be used.

    e. Type of helicopter.

    f. Total number of ropers to exit.

    g. Location of rope station(s) in the aircraft.

    h. Location of safety vehicle.

    i. Location of corpsman.

    j. Other personnel.

3. HRST preparation.

    a. Personnel.

        (1) Corpsman.

        (2) Drivers.

        (3) Working party.

    b. Formation time.

    c. Type of transportation.

    d. HRST time.

    e. Number of sticks.

    f. Number of operations.

    g. Exit sequence, by name.

    h. Safety checks (HRST master/assistant HRST master).

4. HRST training area.

    a. Location (map).

    b. Aerial photograph.

c. Obstacles on/near HRST training area.

d. Flight plan.

e. Exit point.

5. Actions in the loading area.

a. Muster.

b. Equipment and safety check.

c. Loading order and seating arrangement.

d. Review HRST commands/hand-and-arm signals.

6. Actions in the helicopter.

a. Secure seatbelts, unbuckle on HRST master's signal only.

b. Watch for HRST master's signals.

7. Actions on the fast rope.

a. Maintain eye contact with the HRST master at all times prior to beginning a descent.

b. Make deliberate movements toward the rope station while maintaining a hand hold in the helicopter at all times.

c. Grasp the rope firmly (never jump for the rope) as you approach the rope station.

d. Control descent speeds and brake two-thirds of the distance down to avoid landing on another roper or injuring yourself.

e. Look down at the deck and the roper below you while descending.

f. Spread feet shoulder-width apart when you are 3 to 5 feet from the deck and prepare to land.

8. Actions on the deck.

a. Move rapidly away from the rope upon landing. If you are unsteady upon landing or if you fall, immediately roll to your side and away from the rope to prevent injury from following ropers.

b. Pull the rope to the position indicated by the crew chief during the aircrew brief if you are the last roper on the deck and the rope is not being pulled in or jettisoned.

c. Move to the assembly area.

9. Zone control.

a. Radio call sign.

b. Frequency/alternate frequency.

c. Visual signals/air panels.

d. Radio check prior to operation.

e. Actions for radio failure.

10. Malfunctions.

If the roper becomes hung and cannot complete the fast rope, the HRST master requests that the aircraft commander move to a place where he can safely lower the hung roper to the deck. If the roper is hung just below the helicopter, the HRST master requests that the aircraft commander lower the helicopter to about 10 feet above the deck and the HRST master pulls the hung roper back inside the helicopter.

HELICOPTER SPIE BRIEF

1. Hold muster and prepare a passenger manifest.

2. General operations information.

    a. HRST master.

    b. SIO.

    c. Area for HRST operations.

    d. Type of HRST and method to be used.

    e. Type of helicopter.

    f. Total number of ropers in each stick.

    g. Location of rope station(s) in the aircraft.

    h. Location of safety vehicle.

    i. Location of corpsman.

    j. Other personnel.

3. HRST preparation.

    a. Personnel.

        (1) Corpsman.

        (2) Drivers.

        (3) Working party.

    b. Formation time.

    c. Type of transportation.

    d. HRST time.

    e. Number of sticks.

    f. Number of operations.

    g. Safety checks (HRST master/assistant HRST master).

4. HRST training area.

    a. Location (map).

    b. Aerial photograph.

c. Obstacles on/near HRST training area.

d. Flight plan.

5. Actions in the loading area.

   a. Muster.

   b. Equipment and safety check.

   c. Loading order.

   d. Review HRST commands/hand-and-arm signals.

6. Actions on the SPIE.

   a. The uppermost roper maintains eye contact with the HRST master during extraction, flight, and descent and repeats all commands that come from the HRST master to the ropers below.

   b. Maintain eye contact with the deck while descending.

   c. Move legs in a bicycle-like movement while descending to circulate blood.

7. Actions on the deck

   a. Move out from under higher ropers immediately upon contact the deck.

   b. Once on the deck, move to the briefed position.

   c. Do not disconnect your primary and secondary anchor devices until the helicopter is sitting on the deck.

   d. Move rapidly away from the SPIE rope upon dismounting.

8. Zone control.

   a. Radio call sign.

   b. Frequency/alternate frequency.

   c. Visual signals/air panels.

   d. Radio check prior to operation.

   e. Actions for radio failure.

JACOB'S LADDER BRIEF

1. Hold muster and prepare a passenger manifest.

2. General operations information.

    a. HRST master.

    b. SIO.

    c. Area for Jacob's ladder operations.

    d. Type of HRST and method to be used.

    e. Type of helicopter.

    f. Total number of climbers in each stick.

    g. Location of safety boats for water/waterborne extraction.

    h. Location of safety vehicle.

    i. Location of corpsman.

    j. Other personnel.

3. HRST preparation.

    a. Personnel.

        (1) Corpsman.

        (2) Safety swimmers.

        (3) Communications operators.

        (4) Drivers.

        (5) Working party.

    b. Formation time.

    c. Type of transportation.

    d. HRST time.

    e. Number of sticks.

    f. Number of operations.

    g. Safety checks (HRST master/assistant HRST master).

4. HRST training area.

    a. Location (map).

    b. Aerial photograph.

    c. Obstacles on/near HRST training area.

    d. Water temperature.

    e. Sea state.

    f. Flight plan.

5. Action in the loading area.

    a. Muster.

    b. Equipment and safety check.

    c. Loading order.

    d. Review HRST commands/hand-and-arm signals.

6. Actions on the ladder

    a. Understand and comply with all safety and emergency procedures.

    b. Climbers must avoid contact with the ladder until it has touched the surface and discharged any static electricity.

    c. Maintain eye contact with the HRST master prior to and throughout ascent.

    d. Never allow more than two climbers on the ladder at one time.

    e. The first climber grasps the ladder with one arm and reach over the ladder with the opposite arm, grasping the opposite side of the ladder. The climber moves up the ladder until his feet are out of the water, but waits to continue the climb until the next climber has grasped the ladder. This helps hold the ladder vertical for the next climber. Climbers should grasp the stringers and not the rungs to prevent the higher climber from stepping on their hands.

7. Actions in the helicopter.

    a. Immediately upon entering the aircraft, be seated and fasten your seat belt.

    b. Unfasten your seat belt only upon the direction of the HRST master or crew chief.

8. Zone control.

    a. Radio call sign.

    b. Frequency/alt frequency.

    c. Visual signals.

    d. Radio check prior to operation.

    e. Actions for radio failure.

APPENDIX B
HRST BRIEF TO AIRCREW

1. Personnel roll call.

   a. HRST master.

   b. Assistant HRST master(s).

   c. SIO.

   d. HRST personnel.

   e. Aircraft commander.

   f. Copilot.

   g. Crew chief.

2. Operational data.

   a. Tactical air request or fragmentary number.

   b. Takeoff time.

   c. Insertion and extraction time.

   d. Location of insertion and extraction.

   e. Hover altitude.

   f. Number of inserts and extracts.

   g. Number of personnel per insert and extracts.

3. Insertion and extraction zone identification.

   a. Grid coordinates.

   b. Characteristics of the zone.

   c. Obstacles near the zone.

   d. Altitude of the zone.

   e. Location of corpsman.

   f. Zone marking.

   g. Control of ramp, doors, and hatches.

4. Organization.

    a. Organization for movement (two or more helicopters).

    b. Number of personnel in helicopter.

    c. Location of SIO, HRST master, and assistant HRST master(s).

    d. Number of rope stations.

    e. Length of rope.

    f. Equipment needed (e.g., gunner's belt, ICS, safety strap).

5. Sequence of event and responsibilities.

    a. Communication.

    b. HRST commands and hand-and-arm signals.

6. Emergency procedures.

    a. Inside the helicopter.

    b. If ropers must abandoning the rope (over both ground and water).

        (1) Personnel on fast rope/rappel.

        (2) Personnel on SPIE rope.

    c. Cut rope procedures.

    d. Hung roper procedures.

APPENDIX C
HRST COMMANDS

HRST commands are a vital link to aircrew coordination and must be thoroughly understood. They are discussed in detail during all preflight briefs. HRST commands are either mandatory or advisory. Whenever possible the challenge-and-reply method of passing and receiving commands is used in order to ensure that the command sent was received. In the event that voice communications is lost, hand-and-arm signals are used.

Mandatory Commands.

Command	User(s)	Meaning
Abort	Any HRST participant	Cease rope operation immediately.
Brake	HRST master to roper	Stop descent and hold position on the rope until cleared to descend.
Check equipment	HRST master to ropers	Check all personnel equipment and that of nearest team member. Give a "thumbs up" or "thumbs down" reply.
Clear for takeoff	Crew chief to aircraft commander	Ropers and personnel are clear of obstacles.
Clear for forward flight	Crew chief to aircraft commander	Ropers and personnel are clear of obstacles. Transition to forward flight can be accomplished safely.
Clear to descend	Crew chief to aircraft commander	Ropers and personnel are clear of obstacles. A controlled vertical descent is recommended.
Cut rope	Aircraft commander to HRST master	A last ditch action to reduce injuries or save lives. This call can only be given by the aircraft commander.
Deploy the rope	Aircraft commander to HRST master	Established in a stable hover. Clear to lower rope to the deck.
Go	HRST master to roper	Begin descent.
Hold	Crew chief to aircraft commander	Maintain a steady helicopter position.
	HRST master to roper	Stop in position. Remain steady.
Hook up	HRST master to roper	Attach snaplink to rope.
First man off	HRST master to aircraft commander	During SPIE extract, signal aircraft commander to note altitude.
Lock in	HRST master to roper	During fast rope, hold position by stepping one foot on top of the other.
Roper ready	HRST master to aircraft commander	During SPIE, receive a "thumbs up" from team leader to begin vertical extract, ready for forward flight, first man off, and first man on deck.
Retrieve or release the rope	Aircraft commander to HRST master	After assurance that ropers are clear of the rope, directs that ropes be pulled into or released from helicopter.
Rope clear	HRST master to aircraft commander	Ropes have either been pulled inside the helicopter, dropped to the deck, or staged by belay man.
Ropers on the deck	HRST master to aircraft commander	During SPIE dismount, last roper has reached the deck and is unhooking.
Rope out	HRST master to aircraft commander	After clearance to deploy the rope, informs aircraft commander that the rope is deployed.
Strap in	Any HRST participant	Take seat and fasten seat belt or safety strap.
Take position	HRST master to roper	Take final position prior to beginning descent (L position for rappel). Grasp the rope for fast rope.
Unbuckle	HRST master to roper	Take final position prior to beginning descent (L position for rappel). Grasp the rope for fast rope. Await further commands from the HRST master.

Advisory Commands.

Command	User(s)	Meaning
Get ready	HRST master to ropers	Approximately 1 minute out; make final personal inspections of equipment.
First man out	HRST master to aircraft commander	Counts out ropers as they begin descent.
Slide: left, right, forward, back, up, or down	Crew chief to aircraft commander.	Directions for the helicopter to position over target area.
3 minutes and 1 minute	Aircraft commander to HRST master	Approximate time to target area.
25 feet, 10 feet, and 5 feet	Crew chief to HRST master to aircraft commander.	During dismount, approximate distance of roper to the deck.

Hand-and-arm Signals.

Command	Meaning
Abort	Slashing motion of right hand across throat.
Emergency	Right hand slapping motion on top of head.
Brake, hold, or lock-in	Clenched fist.
Clear rope or off belay	Rope executes a side straddle hop.
Equipment not good	Thumbs down. Point to bad equipment.
Cut rope	A hacking motion of a hand on the other forearm.
Deploy the rope	Two hands executing a pushing away motion.
Go	Point down the rope.
Ready to lift	Thumbs up followed by upward motion of right palm.
Retrieve rope	Pulling in motion with both arms.
Strap in	Point to seats and motion both fists together at belt buckle.
Slide (direction)	Open palm motion into direction of desired movement.
Take position	Point at rope station.
Unbuckle	Motion both firsts away from belt buckle.
_____ minute(s)	Point to watch, then hold up the number of fingers corresponding to number of minutes.

APPENDIX D
RAPPEL ROPE LOG

A rope log is used to ensure that rope usage is maintained in accordance with the standards established in the rope grading table (see p. 2-2). Inspect rope for damage and excessive wear each time it is deployed and again after each use. Immediately retire all suspect ropes.

Unit rope ID:		NSN:		MFR. Lot No.:	
Manufacturer:		Date Manufactured:		Date in Service:	
Color:	Length:	Diameter:		Type of Rope:	

Date Used	No. Rappels	Type of Rappels	Rope Grade and Comments	Inspector Initials

Page ___ of ___

APPENDIX E
RAPPEL TOWER INSPECTION

The rappel tower must be on a regularly scheduled inspection/maintenance program. The rappel tower inspection checklist should be used to conduct quarterly inspections of the rappel tower. These inspections include, but are not limited to, repair (as required), padding replacement/repair, and replenishment of wood mulch. Inspections and maintenance are performed by command personnel, the base's public works department, or private contract.

Periodically, the tower should be inspected by a qualified engineer (the engineer determines time intervals based on the type of structure, usage, climatic conditions, etc). A copy of the engineer's certification is kept on file. The certification should cover the load test rating of the existing rope anchor points.

Rappel Tower Inspection Checklist.

Yes	No	Conditions
		Is the tower structurally sound?
		Are all open areas (above 4 feet) protected with guardrails?
		Are all guardrails a minimum of 42 inches high and capable of withstanding a side force of 200 pounds?
		Are toe boards installed in all areas where personnel could pass underneath?
		Do all stairs/fixed ladders comply with Occupational Safety and Health Administration standards?
		Do all tower rope stations have three anchor points each?
		Have all rappel rope anchor points been load tested and certified to 5,000 pounds each?
		Have all fast rope anchor points been tested and certified to 5,000 pounds each, per person on the rope (e.g. two ropers on the rope at the same time requires testing to 10,000 pounds each [2 x 5,000 pounds])?
		Are all anchor points in good condition and free of corrosion, sharp edges, burrs, etc.?
		Is the tower deck free of trip/slip hazards (e.g., water, protruding nails/bolts, splinters)?
		Are the rappel wall face and the fast rope area free of protrusions and broken or loose boards?
		Do the tower deck and the stairway tread have a nonskid surface?
		Is there padding on all edges that ropes and/or personnel cross?
		Is the edge padding in good condition and securely fastened?
		Are there any signs of insect infestation?
		Is the landing area free of obstructions and hazards?
		Do the landing areas consist of a cushioning material (recommend: 24-inch deep, noncompressed wood chips or mulch)?
		Has the landing area been loosened up prior to use and, if large number of students are rappelling, loosened up again during training?
		Are all structural areas of the tower that a rappeller might contact during rappel/fast rope operations properly padded?
		Is all structural padding in good condition and securely fastened?
		Are all areas that pose a trip hazard or head hazard marked in yellow?
		Are the tower platform and all rappel rope stations accessible without having to climb over any obstacles (e.g., guardrails, support cables)?

APPENDIX F
TOWER SAFETY BRIEF

1. Type of operation.

2. HRST master.

3. SIO.

4. Range safety officer.

5. Corpsman.

6. Safety vehicle.

7. Tower safety.

   – No smoking within 50 feet of the rope equipment.
   – All rappellers must have helmets and gloves.
   – Roll sleeves down and tuck in blouses.
   – Remove all sharp objects from pockets. Tie rappel seats.
   – No sitting on your rappel seat.
   – If you take the rappel seat off, it must be rechecked.
   – Only one rappeller on the ladder at a time.
   – Once on top only as many rappellers at the station as deemed safe.
   – At no time will you go near the edge of the tower.
   – Identify who is uneasy towards heights.
   – Gear will be checked prior to ascending the tower and before descending.
   – No one will descend without gloves on both hands.
   – Do not step on any ropes.
   – No bounding (except skid).

8. Tower rappel procedures.

   – Before climbing ladder, gear will be checked.
   – All debris must be knocked off of boots.
   – One rappeller climbs at a time.
   – Sound off, "*On ladder.*"
   – Sound off , "*Off ladder.*"
   – Once on top wait until directed to rope station by HRST master.
   – Hook up rappeller.
   – Maintain brake and face towards anchor point.
   – Move to the edge and sound off with name, "*Jones on rappel.*"
   – Form a good L shape and go.
   – Get off of the rope.

9. Belay man procedures.

- Most important safety factor.
- Remove gloves and equipment.
- Pass rope under armpits/strong arm up.
- Stand one arm's length from wall/directly under rappeller for the skid and hell hole.
- Slack (one arm's length). Eyes on the rappeller at all times.
- If rappeller falls, lock out until he can recover or lower slowly to the deck.
- Get the rappeller off the rope.
- Physically change over.

10. Proper rappel techniques.

- Seat hip rappel.
- Keep a good L position.
- Brake out to the 3 o'clock position.
- Positive brakes every 15 feet.
- Watch the ground.

11. Night rappel procedures.

- No talking.
- Sound off only: *"Jones on/off ladder."*
                      "Jones on/off rappel."
                      "Falling."

- Night signals (chem lights).
- HRST master will check for belay man and signal by waving a chem light with a vertical slashing motion in front of the body.
- SIO responds with a vertical slashing motion, from a chem light, in front of the body for *"Go."*
- SIO responds with a horizontal slashing motion in front of the body if the operation is to be *"Aborted."*

12. Proper fast rope techniques.

- Approach rope station on command of the HRST master.
- On command, grasp the rope below the HRST master's hands with your hands and feet.
- On the command of *"Go"*, do a 45 to 90 degree turn away from the HRST master.
- Keep hands at face level.
- Do not wrap feet or legs around the rope.
- Let rope slide between arches of feet.
- Look down at the deck and the roper below you.
- If hands start to burn, apply more foot/knee/hand pressure. **DO NOT LET GO OF THE ROPE.**
- Spread feet (to absorb shock) 3 to 5 feet from the deck and conduct a fast rope landing fall.
- If you loose your balance let go of the rope and roll out of the way.
- Demonstrate lock-in procedures.

13. Hung roper.

    – Tower retrieval.
    – Instructor will retrieve.

14. Injury.

    – Minor.
    – Serious.
    – Fatality.

APPENDIX G
GLOSSARY

Acronyms and Abbreviations

AFSOC . . . . Air Force Special Operations Command
AGL . . . . .above ground level
FRIES . . . . Fast Rope Insertion Extraction System
HRST . . . . helicopter rope suspension techniques
ICS . . . . internal communications system
LPP . . . . life preserver personal

MALS . . . . .Marine Aviation Logistics Squadron
NAVAIR. . . . . Naval Air Systems Command
NDI . . . . .nondestructive inspection
NVD . . . . night vision device
PFD . . . . personal flotation device
POL. . . . . .petroleum, oils, and lubricants
SIO . . . . .safety insert officer
SOP . . . . standing operating procedure
SPIE . . . . . special patrol insertion and extraction

HRST Terminology

belay/brake. In HRST, a method to control or stop the uncontrolled descent of a roper.

bight. A bend in the rope that does not cross itself.

fast rope. A technique that inserts Marines into small areas from a helicopter. The ropers slide down the rope and are not attached to it.

fast rope landing. A fast rope landing technique used to prevent injury during a rapid descent.

figure eight assault descenders. An aluminum-alloy or steel device that roughly resembles the number eight. A descender is used when rappelling with heavy loads.

helicopter rope suspension training (HRST) master. A Marine trained and certified to instruct rappelling, fast rope, and SPIE operations.

line. An 11 millimeter diameter rope that is used in rappelling.

loop. A bend in the line/rope in which the line/rope crosses itself.

pigtails. The short length left at the end of a rope after tying a knot or coiling a rope.

rope station. The point on a static tower or helicopter where ropers are expected to execute their descent.

round turn. Wrapping the rope around a specific object such as a post, rail, or pipe so that it has a 360 degree contact. The running end leaves the object in the same direction as the standing end.

running end. The free or working end of a rope.

sling rope. An 11 millimeter rappel line that is approximately 12 to 15 feet long and burned on both ends. It is used to construct the rappel seat and safety harness.

special patrol insertion and extraction (SPIE). A method to insert and/or extract troops by helicopter from water or rough terrain conditions.

webbing. A flat rope made of nylon or polyester. Its most common usage is for slings and harnesses. The sizes used most often are 1-inch and 2-inch webbing. It is made in two forms: flat and tubular.

whipping. A wrapping or binding of light cord on the end of a line to prevent it from unraveling.

APPENDIX H
REFERENCES AND RELATED PUBLICATIONS

Navy Publications

Naval Air Systems Command (NAVAIR)

13-45-2   Special Patrol Insertion/Extraction (SPIE) System

Naval Warfare Publication (NWPs)

3-22.5-CH-46   CH-46 Tactical Manual

3-2.5-CH-53   CH-53 Tactical Manual

3-22.5-UH-1   UH-1 Tactical Manual

Office of the Chief of Naval Operations Instruction (OPNAVINST)

3710.7   NATOPS General Flight and Operating Instructions

Commander Naval Special Warfare Command Instruction (COMNAVSPECWARCOMINST)

3000.3   Naval Special Warfare Air Operations Manual

Marine Corps Publications

Marine Corps Orders (MCO)

P5102.1   Marine Corps Ground Mishap Investigation and Reporting Manual

3500.27   Operatingal Risk Management (OPM)

3500.42   Marine Corps Helicopter Rope Suspension Training Policy (HRST) and Program Administration

Marine Corps Reference Publication (MCRP)

5-12C   Marine Corps Supplement to the Department of Defense Dictionary of Military and Associated Terms